BEING
JOHN STANKEVITCH

BEING
JOHN STANKEVITCH

To Eddie

LEAGUE PUBLICATIONS LTD

League Publications Ltd
Wellington House
Briggate
Brighouse HD6 1DN
England

First published in Great Britain in 2011
by League Publications Ltd

www.totalrl.com

A CIP catalogue record for this book is available
from the British Library

ISBN: 978-1-901347-23-4

Designed and Typeset by League Publications Limited
Printed by Antony Rowe – CPI

Cover picture: Rugby League Photos

To Kerry, Sian and Oliver. Your love has given me
the strength to come through the negative times.

Acknowledgments

Without the help and support from a number of people, I wouldn't have been where I am today.

My granddad, Philip Welbourne, is no longer with me in body, but with me every day in spirit. He was so proud of what I achieved as a player and played every game with me, but unfortunately passed away only a few weeks after I joined Rochdale Hornets. I'm sure that he has seen the good work I have done and continue to do at Rochdale as I build my coaching career in the game. I'm sure I'll make him just as proud again.

Also, my mum, dad, sister and nan, who have been with me every step of the way, with every pass of the ball and with every tackle I made. I couldn't have got here without their undivided attention and commitment to helping me fulfil my goals. I hope my memories do them justice.

Last, but certainly not least, to Kerry, Sian and Oliver, who are everything to me. Their support in difficult times has never been in question and has always given me a reason to continue to fight on against adversity. It is through them I always see the positives. I hope this autobiography serves its purpose for us all.

I'd also like to thank the rest of my family, however disjointed we are, they have all played their part. And to Tim Butcher and Martyn Sadler at League Publications, who had the confidence in me to leave me to write this autobiography entirely on my own! Thanks fellas!

And also everybody I have come across in this fantastic game who has helped me to keep moving forward - players I have played with, kitmen that have supplied my clothing, coaches that have made me a better player, support staff that have kept me motivated, fans that have supported me, and working colleagues that continue to help me realise my dreams.

I thank you all.   JOHN STANKEVITCH

FOREWORD
Ian Millward

WHEN I WAS ASKED TO PUT A FOREWORD to John's book I was firstly humbled but then engulfed with some special thoughts and moments in both our lives.

Reflecting on John's journey in rugby league is a stark realisation to all aspiring sportsman of the highs and goals that we can dream of and also the cruelty of sport which can see dreams evaporate before our eyes, out of our control.

The first time I met John was in March 2000 when I was being introduced as the new St Helens head coach, I addressed a galaxy of stars – current and former internationals and also budding youngsters who were striving to fulfil their dreams of becoming a regular player with one of the biggest clubs in rugby league, where a regular spot could hopefully give the opportunity to win trophies, international honours and financial stability. John was one of these youngsters.

John did not disappoint anyone in 2000, his enthusiasm and respect towards the rewards that lay ahead for him and the team is what keeps senior professionals appreciative of their position in a team, and coaches gaining satisfaction of seeing a young player grow in confidence and stature.

When I picked John in early 2000 for his first derby game against Wigan he was so excited; we won, he played well and I continued to pick him for the following weeks. John was strong enough to say after a couple of games "hey coach I would love more minutes". He was right and due to him making teammates, himself and the coach accountable we had a healthy competition between all players.

John had the rugby league world at his feet; he was an integral part of the St Helens team winning all three trophies on offer: Challenge Cup, Super League and the World Club Championship. As a wide running second-rower he had agility alongside deceptive footwork at the defensive line and the ability to pass and offload – he had plenty of strings to his bow. In 2003 I thought: "come on Great Britain coach our man is ready to step up to international honours"; however sport can be cruel and offers no guarantees.

Following an illegal incident in the play-offs in 2003 John's subsequent injury saw his exit from St Helens and ultimately as a player from the game.

With a family to support, financial commitments and lack of job offers due to his injury, John was now facing his biggest challenge. How many times must he have thought "why me" when a former teammate won an accolade or trophy, one can only imagine how tough it must have been for him and his partner Kerry. The attributes he possessed – enthusiasm, commitment, hard work, attention to detail -were now used in a different arena – life.

Not only is John's story a reminder of the pitfalls that can happen in sport but it is a story of how he has stood tall, faced the future and emerged wanting to help and mentor young players who want to play rugby league, encouraging them to enjoy the game and unselfishly helping them to try and obtain their dreams and goals. This I believe is John's great achievement – not playing in front of 75,000 people at Old Trafford – his ability and dedication to get on with the job and help others is a truly rare quality.

When John spoke with me and asked me write some words for his book he was frantically getting from his day job to an evening training session as a head coach. I said "John, you always seem in a hurry." He replied" "yeah, we are not all lucky enough to have a full-time job in sport, but we are both lucky to be involved in it regardless of our time schedule."

Thanks for the reminder John and thanks for being part of rugby league history, and its future.

IAN MILLWARD

Prologue

IT WAS FRIDAY 3RD OCTOBER 2003. ST HELENS travelled to the JJB Stadium to take on our deadliest rivals, Wigan, in an elimination semi-final. A week before I had been named in the full Great Britain squad for the first time. We were the reigning champions, but our luck ran out. We were soundly beaten by a battle-hardened team.

It was a night I will never forget and a night that was the beginning of the end for me as a player.

Over the course of the next few weeks, we visited an expert physician numerous times to get a diagnosis and to prepare for an operation or a schedule of treatment and rehabilitation. I was given nerve conduction tests, physical examinations and scans on my shoulder and, eventually, after approximately a month, I was given some news I wasn't expecting. The doctor sat me down in his office and explained I had suffered severe nerve damage through my shoulder as a result of the impact of a collision and the likelihood of me playing the game ever again was very slim. In fact he recommended there and then that I should retire from playing. I didn't get emotional, I didn't shout and bawl, I didn't ask questions, I just sat and did nothing. I couldn't really take in what I had just been told.

I was only 24-years-old. I was determined that the damning verdict given on my condition wouldn't see the end of me as a player. In fact, I couldn't let it be the end of me, because I had nothing else to do, and nothing else that I wanted to do.

Chapter 1

I BEGAN PLAYING RUGBY LEAGUE BY complete coincidence.

My accidental path to being a professional player began as a nine year-old at my local team Widnes Tigers. We had recently moved house from the Upton part of Widnes to the Hough Green area of the same town. In reality it was simply a move across a road; the houses were probably 200 yards apart. But the move meant I was closer to the local playing fields. Living in Upton, and as a young boy, my parents were reluctant to let me cross the main road to travel the three hundred or so yards to the fields. Once we had relocated there was no need to ask permission to 'travel' to those fields.

It was early on a Sunday morning back in 1989 and I had gone onto the field with a childhood friend of mine to kick around a football. To get to the football pitches at the top end of the field, we had to walk past a few pitches with unusual shaped football goals. At that age, I wasn't aware of what these H shaped structures represented, as I was heavily into football and was an avid Liverpool supporter, but being a young impressionable and no doubt mischievous young lad, I was fairly curious as to what the group of boys around my age were doing on this pitch, running around with an unusual shaped ball. As we passed the half way point of the first pitch, one of the grown ups that were watching this activity called over my friend and we both began to walk towards him. We were told that the group were short of players for a match later that morning and asked whether we would like to play. Whether through instinct or stupidity, I immediately agreed to give it a go.

I don't remember anything at all about that particular game; however, it must have been something I enjoyed, as it was the beginning of a passion for the game of rugby league that has been ongoing for 21 years. Not long after starting to play the game, I began watching the local professional team with my granddad. We would drive from my grandparents' house in Upton and would park near the Albion Pub at the top of Lowerhouse Lane and then walk the 150 yards or so to Naughton Park, home of Widnes Rugby League Club. One of the first games I can recall watching was the Championship decider of 1989 between Widnes and Wigan. I was an observer from the half way point of the touchline, and the view was fantastic, so much so that when Martin Offiah would receive the ball on his wing, I felt I was in touching distance of him. I had so many idols from that team that it would be inappropriate to only mention a few of the players, who I consider to be League legends. If I were to pinpoint any particular moment from my childhood that lit the fuse for me to strive to emulate those players, I'd have to say it was that day. Running onto the field at full time to ask for the 'tie ups' of your heroes was a moment to savour.

I watched Widnes many more times after that fantastic occasion in 1989 and I suppose it was the atmosphere at those home games that gave me the desire to play there myself one day. It wouldn't be too long after that I achieved that goal when I represented Lancashire against Yorkshire at under-11s for the junior War of the Roses at Naughton Park as a curtain raiser to the full inter-county fixture.

I wouldn't say I was considered a stand out player by any means. I was hard working and would regularly top the tackle counts but I was never a player who would break the line and run the full length of the field to finish under the posts. Not that that ever held me back in terms of junior representation. From age nine to eleven I played for Widnes Tigers before joining another Widnes based club, Halton Hornets, where I played until I was fifteen. For my final season in the junior game, I joined a club from outside the Halton borough, Golborne Parkside, and it was here that I would have my best season as an amateur player. I had represented the Widnes town team at every age group and I had also represented South Lancashire and the full Lancashire junior sides. But by the age of 15, I was beginning to get slightly nervous as to where my potential Rugby League career was heading. There were other players of a similar standard to me beginning to get noticed by the local professional clubs, and I was starting to get disheartened that my name never seemed to crop up in conversation. The scouts would regularly come to watch the games I was playing in, but with a glance towards them every now and again throughout the games, I would never see them speaking to my parents as they seemed to do with the other lads. St Helens, Widnes, Wigan, Oldham, Warrington, Leigh, they were all there.

The move to Golborne Parkside was forced upon me in many ways due to circumstances at my previous club, Halton Hornets. The players had lost a bit of interest, we were having very low numbers at training, and although we were one of the best teams around in that age group, there didn't seem to be the same desire to succeed from the rest of the players. Eventually, the team folded, and a group of us decided to join Golborne, with a major reason being that we knew the coach, Terry Byrne. Terry had coached some of us with Lancashire and was a good coach as well as a really nice bloke, but in all honesty the major reason for me joining Golborne was the location. Situated between Wigan, St Helens and Warrington, and with a sound history as a club, I thought that if I were to attract interest from those top clubs I would need to be playing in the immediate area. As luck would have it, the team I was joining were pretty good as well. I settled in right away and attained a regular starting spot in the front row. We went on to win the Lancashire Trophy in that season by beating the all-conquering Wigan St Pats side, which included about a dozen lads who had already signed professional terms with Wigan.

Arguably my best performance as an amateur was for Lancashire against Yorkshire later in that season in 1996, as a 16 year-old. I played in the front row that day at Leigh and walked away with the man of the match shield. I had been told by quite a few people that this was possibly last-chance saloon for us if we weren't already attached to a professional club, as there was likely to be a whole host of scouts coming to the game. I was obviously nervous, but on that particular day, whether it is fate or not, I had the game of my life and was the dominant player on the field. Not long after, my dad started getting phone calls from different clubs in our immediate area.

Oldham, Rochdale, and Leigh were all interested in speaking to me, as well as my home-town club Widnes. At the time, Widnes were not enjoying the same success as when I began watching the team in 1989 but, nonetheless, I wanted to sign for them, of course. My dad thought it would be right to be courteous with the other interested parties and also speak to them, which we did, but I always knew that I wanted to sign for my home-town club. I remember going down to Naughton Park on a cold Tuesday evening to speak to them. The way things worked in those days, you met the scout who had arranged the meeting, and he would show you up into the head coach's office. At the time, that was Doug Laughton. Anybody who knows anything about the game knows that Doug Laughton's name is legendary in rugby league and he has had, during his time as a coach, enormous success.

On this particular evening, I will pay him the respect he deserves and just say that he was slightly distracted. George Sadler, who was the man to scout me for Widnes, led me and my dad upstairs in the old

Widnes offices at the clock end of Naughton Park. We sat for a moment outside Doug's office whilst 'Sagga' popped his head around the office door to say that we had arrived. 'Sagga' then ushered us into the office, where Doug was sat in a big leather chair with his feet on his desk and a telephone in his hand. I was certainly surprised with the scene that confronted me and, especially, the fact I was not acknowledged by the coach. We waited for a good five minutes for the telephone conversation to end, at which point we were asked by Doug what we wanted.

We were back in my dad's car within one minute and on our way home. Whether the meeting hadn't been scheduled correctly or whether the situation was handled that way by Doug and 'Sagga' to show me I was just a small part of a big organisation, I'm not sure, but I wasn't too comfortable with what had happened, and my dad certainly wasn't having me treated that way. When the reality of the situation had sunk in properly, I was incredibly disappointed and felt that my opportunity had passed by, but the following evening my dad received a phone call from John Myler, who had previously played for Widnes and was now coaching the youngsters at St Helens. John had heard about my 'talks' with Widnes and had already been resigned to the fact that I would definitely sign with them, but he had then heard the situation had changed. Between the two of them, they arranged for me to go to St Helens on the Thursday evening to discuss signing for Saints.

On arrival, I was met by John, Tom Ellard and Mal

Kay, two of the Saints directors. My immediate impression was one of professionalism. The appearance of John, Tom and Mal was very smart indeed and I was made to feel very welcome from the moment I arrived. I was shown around Knowsley Road, shown every nook and cranny and I was introduced to everybody, from the tea lady to the chairman. What made the meeting extra special was that I was shown into the changing rooms and I was fortunate enough to meet with some of the players. I knew from that initial half-hour introduction I would be signing for Saints. I hadn't even discussed the terms of my contract. For me, money wasn't the most important thing about becoming a professional. The opportunity to improve my game at one of the best clubs in the division was an opportunity not to be missed. When it came to discussing my contract, and my future at the club, the talks were very open and honest, and I was told that I would have to work very hard and be committed to progressing through the ranks from Academy to Alliance and then hopefully to the first team. I suppose, it is the job of the directors to make sure that the young players are fully aware of just how hard it is going to be to progress, and I was left clear in my mind that it would be one hell of a challenge.

When it finally came to discussing my contract terms, I remember my jaw almost hitting the floor, as I was reading figures of fifty thousand plus. At the age of sixteen, it's not often that you see such figures and it was incredibly exciting to have a piece of paper in front of me with my name next to those amounts. The figures took some explaining and, to be honest, a lot of the conversation went over my head and would have to be explained to me later by my dad. The actual contract was very heavily incentive based, and my guaranteed money was only two thousand pounds a year for five years. So in effect, ten thousand rather than £50,000! The rest of the money would be paid in incentives such as three thousand pounds after every ten first-team games and seven-and-a-half thousand for winning a Great Britain cap. Hardly achievable for a sixteen year-old boy, but nonetheless, I signed the contract and was happy with every facet of what I had seen and been told.

Once our 'official meeting' was over, I said my goodbyes to Mr Ellard and Mr Kay, and John Myler accompanied myself and dad downstairs and back to our car. All that was left for John to tell me was when training started, and with that in mind, we made our way back to Widnes. Once we arrived home, I was straight on the phone to some of my closer school friends to tell them the good news. One particular friend of mine, Paul, had just begun working as an apprentice electrician for the sum of £70 per week, and I remember vividly at the time that I had had a slight snigger at the career path he had chosen. I could, of course, afford that reaction after I had signed for St Helens to become a professional rugby league player! As things would eventually work out, Paul now owns his own electrical company and has done very well for himself and he should be very pleased with the path he chose to take. Not everybody is lucky enough to get the opportunity to play sport for money and should you have a passion for something, whatever it is, you should be encouraged to pursue that passion.

My reason for sniggering at the time when I learnt that my mate would be doing hard graft for £70 per week was that I felt that he could have gone and got a 'regular' job in a local shop and earned double the pay packet. That was me, very short sighted on the future, but I had no reason to think otherwise, because at that moment in time, I was a St Helens Rugby League professional. Even now, writing that tag line 'St Helens Rugby League professional' sounds incredibly exciting. But at the time, although it sounded great, it wasn't necessarily true. As a young lad, you try to show off and be the 'big man' and will do anything you can to get the attention you feel you deserve. There's a slight arrogance and swagger about you and I definitely had that, because I was made to feel special and I was watching first-team players being adored on match days by the fans. I wanted a piece of the action.

What, in fact, I was, was a 'semi professional' rugby league player. I wasn't on a full-time contract and my wage was just two thousand pounds per year, but with that, I had the opportunity to play matches and increase that by a minimum of fifteen pounds if we lost or a maximum of thirty-five if we won. That was in the academy. For the reserves, the minimum match lose bonus was forty pounds and the win bonus was seventy-five and the better players were encouraged by those bonuses to progress as quickly as possible through the ranks. Of course, being a young lad, excited by money and what money could buy I wanted to progress through the ranks very quickly. For me, though, one of the most exciting parts of signing for Saints was receiving my kitbag full of shorts, T-shirts, sweaters, socks and rain jackets, all embroidered with the famous St Helens logo. Something to be proud of, things that are player issue only. You know when you wear those items that you are part of a special group of people, and that is exactly how you feel when you are in the company of your teammates in full training gear. I was focussed, single minded and hungry for success and I had achieved my first goal of getting on the ladder's first rung. I had signed a contract to play rugby league and the only way was up. I wasn't going to let anything get in my way, and I was already focussing on my next goal, becoming a regular for the club's academy side.

Chapter 2

WITH A REGULAR 'TAKE HOME' WAGE OF just over forty pounds per week, without additional match bonuses, I needed to start earning a little bit more money so I could learn to drive in order to get to training and back from Widnes. As all young lads do, I relied in those early years very heavily on my dad, and he would regularly finish shifts at work, rush home for a quick bite to eat, and then drive me to St Helens, sometimes waiting until 9pm in the evening to take me home. I was getting older and wanted to become more independent. I had left school in the June of 1996 and enrolled into college in Widnes, but in the early weeks of college I felt very strongly that study just didn't fit with the pathway I was taking.

I was at college all of two months before taking the decision to leave and get a full-time job which would give me the money to learn to drive and hopefully buy a car. At the time it seemed an inspired decision as, within six months, I had learnt to drive and was in the process of looking for my first vehicle, which would give me the extra independence that I wanted so much. Study had been forgotten completely, although I did think I would like to eventually return to education in order to take advantage of the good GCSE grades I came out of school with. Although school wasn't my number one focus around exam time, I had studied hard enough to pass all ten of my chosen GCSE subjects, and although I certainly wasn't the brightest in my classes, I could hold my own in the top sets of those subjects. A little bit more application and dedication, as I was told by a few teachers, and I could have been a straight A student. But those same teachers knew that my passion was for rugby and they quite understood when it came to homework tasks I handed in incomplete due to training.

On leaving college, I got a job in a local sportswear shop and although the money wasn't great for a full-time job, it was enough for me to start living independently, my social life was improving no end, and I was beginning to enjoy the start of my adult life. I was a weekend regular in local legendary nightspot 'Top of the Town' and I was training every night of the week up at St Helens. I was occupied for most of the time, and this kept me level headed and grounded during a time when a lot of young people lose focus and direction in their own lives. I knew exactly where I wanted to be and where I wanted to go, and I was thoroughly enjoying the camaraderie of my teammates. The majority were local lads from St Helens, Warrington, and Widnes and we were a talented group when we put our mind to it. We had some very committed coaching staff working with us and my own game went from strength to strength under the guidance of those coaches.

One of my first memories of training up at Saints was my meeting with a Mr Jack Penman. To this day, when I speak to old teammates and we begin chatting about our days in the academy and Jack's name crops up, we all let out a groan of forgotten pain. Jack was a fantastic bloke and is the person to whom I attribute my physical progression during the first 18 months of my contract. Jack is renowned locally and nationally as a successful bodybuilder and he was the man tasked with improving the physical condition of every player on Saints' books, from academy to first team. By the time I was seventeen I had never had the opportunity to do any weight lifting, and I had no idea about diets and healthy eating plans, but Jack certainly put me on the path to knowing a thing or two about those topics. Jack Penman, weights, diets and strength together equalled 'pain'. I have never known pain like it in all my life. He would have us on so many tablets that we would rattle when we walked. Amino acids, desiccated liver, kelp, creatine and protein shakes were the order of the day. Take that alongside four heavy, and I mean heavy, weight sessions a week and you go from being thirteen stones to fifteen stones within six months. Well that's certainly what happened to me. I turned from a boy to a man with the guidance of Jack and those sessions of lifting more than my own bodyweight not only made me physically strong but also mentally strong, something which is a major part of any professional athlete.

In all my time involved in Rugby League, I have never cheated and taken anything illegal, I have always believed that people achieve what they set out to if they believe in themselves and work incredibly hard to get there. I have no time for people who take shortcuts or cheat the systems and those that do only have themselves to blame when things go wrong.

The environment I was around at St Helens was one of blood, sweat and tears, and an incredible work ethic and I don't think it is any coincidence that so many young players matured from academy stars through to regular first-teamers having worked alongside Jack. The other coaches I worked under in the early part of my career also had an impact in helping me to achieve my own goals. John Myler, who was to be my first academy coach, gave me a steely determination as well as keeping me grounded and level headed. John was the type of coach to tell you when you played well, but also to give it to you when you played poorly, and it is this honest and up front approach that I use within my own coaching to this day. Nick Halafihi was also an academy coach of mine, and had an entirely different approach. He was quite punishing as a bloke, and although he wasn't as approachable as John Myler, his strictness gave the players direction both on and off the field. I also played under ex-Saints first-teamer Dave Lyon, and former Wigan forward Brian Case, as well as legendary Mike Gregory. Every coach I have worked with has given me something completely different that I have taken and used in both my rugby life and my personal life and I am indebted to the systems I came through at Saints. The system itself was perfect for what I needed at that particular time. I obviously had one eye on the first team squad and of course that was my ultimate goal, but I felt that before I even considered myself good enough for that level, I had to be a decent player with the academy and the reserve teams.

As my physique changed, I found myself moved from the front row and into the back row, and I began to change as a player. It was noticeable that I was gaining an extra yard of pace and also my footwork was improving no end, and the coaching staff decided I would be more of a threat a little wider of the ruck. Couple that with the fact that we had some big blokes in our side, then I was more suited to playing on the fringes and running off our halfbacks. I probably played a season and a half intermittently in the academy before I was moved permanently up to the alliance, as it was known then. The alliance back in 1998 was a competition for first teamers that were not getting selected, for players returning from injury, and for the more talented of the academy who the coaches felt could handle the step up. I certainly wasn't the first, and definitely not the second, and on seeing the size of some of the players I'd be playing with, I wasn't sure that I was in the third category! But when turning out for the alliance, I was always lucky enough to have some 'protection' from some of the bigger boys. Whether this was something the coaches had told them or whether they were doing it out of good nature, I'm not sure, but I was indebted at times to Vila Matautia and Apollo Perelini, who more than watched my back.

As an eighteen year-old playing against physically

matured men is quite a big ask of a young lad, but I felt I handled myself well and I was always aware there was likely to be a player on the opposition side who would want to make a name for himself by bashing the young lad. This actually happened quite a few times against my hometown club, but I like to think I was too smart for the players that tried it on. When I appeared for the alliance, I equipped myself reasonably well and well enough to remain in the alliance rather than go back to the academy. The coaches must have agreed as I never returned back to the academy once I'd left them.

During my second season in the alliance, which would have been 1999, there was a lot of talk of giving me a first-team call up. Ellery Hanley was now the first team coach after the departure of Shaun McRae, but I was always a little sceptical whenever I was linked with the first team. I didn't think I had done enough to warrant another move up the ladder, but at the end of the season, when I was awarded the alliance player of the year, things certainly looked more positive for me. I was still however only on a contract guaranteeing me two thousand pounds per year although with match bonuses I would say that I would have been picking up more likely three, big money I know. I knew I had played quite well that season, and I was promised when I first signed a contract that if things were progressing for me on the field, then things would be happening for me off the field. In other words, I would be financially rewarded. I was obviously disappointed this wasn't happening as I had been told three years earlier, but both Tom Ellard and Mal Kay had gone from the club and new directors were in place.

I'm sure the new directors weren't aware of the conversations that took place between every young kid and the previous board. However, this wasn't a concern of mine and all I wanted was what I felt I deserved for my performances. So, when I was approached by Huddersfield Giants not long after our end-of-season awards with a £25,000 contract, car and house, my head turned a little to say the least.

As a headstrong young man, my immediate reaction was to go to the board of directors and plead with them to be released in order to take advantage of this fantastic opportunity. Almost nineteen years-old with the chance of earning two thousand pounds per month, not including match bonuses, was too good an opportunity to turn down. But as with all club directors I have ever met, they stood rigid and wouldn't let me leave the club. I pleaded my case for them to match what I had been offered at Huddersfield, and they refused flat. They said I hadn't earned the contract that was on the table from Huddersfield, although I made the point that the offer was showing the potential that other clubs believed I had. Anyway, I was ushered out of the boardroom and into the car park with not even the chance of a contract discussion. I was told to get on with my Saints career and concentrate on getting into Ellery's squad.

I was immensely disappointed as you can imagine, but I didn't have a legal leg to stand on. The rules at the time meant any player under the age of 24 who wanted to leave to join another club would be subject to a transfer fee set by the club with whom he was contracted. I didn't hold much hope that Saints would let me go for a nominal fee. One thing that my mum says when things do go a person's way, is that things happen for a reason, and as it worked out, the Saints board did come back and give me a new contract for eight thousand pounds. At the time, I wasn't at all impressed by the offer and I was very close to turning it down and asking for a release from my contract, but the offer coincided with a conversation I had with Ellery Hanley who told me he wanted me to train full time from November 1999.

I was ecstatic, though this would mean me giving up my job in the sports shop. It took all of five seconds for me to decide what to do. Although the basic contract salary wasn't huge, it was heavily incentive based like my first Saints contract, only the incentives this time around were individually match based. For each appearance I would earn five hundred pounds! I went home later that afternoon and sat down with my parents and we discussed my options. The outcome was fairly straightforward from all of us. I was going to sign the contract and throw everything into this opportunity. I called the Chairman and I agreed to sign. In all honesty, I never thought at the time that the coming season would be anything other than an opportunity to learn all about what happens at first-team level. I thought I might get the odd game here or there, possibly play in some friendly fixtures or play against the lower division teams in the early rounds of the Challenge Cup. I was in for a shock.

Chapter 3

I BEGAN TRAINING WITH THE FIRST TEAM-squad in early November 1999 and it was an honour to be there with some world-renowned stars of the game. I was lucky enough to be welcomed by the squad and I quickly adapted to a complete change in the team culture from what I had previously been used to at alliance and academy level. The members of the squad were all full time, but as with the majority of professional sports, full time didn't actually mean full time in terms of the general public's working hours. The time spent on the training field and in the gym was filled with activity that simply could not be maintained over the length of a normal working day. The intensity of training as a full-time sportsman was overwhelming at times and it took a lot to adapt.

The guidance from the coaching staff and the players was fantastic and the experienced professionals within the group always led from the front. The field sessions were very tough and my first few months with the first team were spent up at Edge Hill University in Ormskirk where we were exposed to some of the harshest winter conditions I have known. The facility was 'open plan' and hitting tackle shields on the rugby pitch in gale-force winds and rain was probably the last thing I was expecting to do now I was a first-teamer. I'd always considered myself to be relatively mentally tough, but the early months with

Ellery's team was an eye opener, to say the very least.

It was no coincidence these players had been so successful. The majority of the sessions were physically very draining which, as a rugby player knows, is part and parcel of pre-season training, but the mental conditioning we put ourselves through is what makes the champion teams. The ability to keep pushing on through the adversity you are faced with; to keep turning up the day after a tough hills session when you wake in the morning with legs that don't want to get out of bed. That is the making of the best teams and the best individuals. I suppose, having one of the greatest ever rugby league players watching over you gives you that extra incentive not to fail and I certainly wanted to impress Ellery in every way I could.

I wasn't the most gifted of trainers, never the quickest, fittest, strongest or most agile, but I had a great determination to succeed at what I wanted to do. I had a method of challenging myself in every session, whether that be in the gym, on the training field or on the running track. There were some great role models within the team but as I had made my way through the academy and alliance as a back rower, I quickly looked to challenge Chris Joynt. If I wanted to take things a little easier, I could have chosen an easier opponent such as one of the younger lads from the Alliance that had made the step up to the first-team squad with me. The likes of Mark Edmondson, Mike Bennett or Tim Jonkers would have been the lads to try and challenge. But my method of thinking was a little more complex than that. Joynty was the club captain at the time and I judged that if I was to become a member of the match-day seventeen I would like to be putting pressure on the best back rower we had. If I could chase him down on the track, last longer than him on the field drills and lift more than him in the gym, then it would make the coaching staff sit up and take note.

It was a lot more difficult than I thought it would be. I had a little bit of arrogance about me and signing as a full-time player certainly gives your confidence a boost, but comparing my early results to those of Joynty's were a bit embarrassing to say the least. I continued to challenge him in whatever the activity was and I like to think that during my time with the squad, over the over years I was playing in the first team I made a bit of progress on him!

To be coached early in my career by a man of Ellery Hanley's stature was a dream come true. I had watched him play for Wigan at Naughton Park back in 1989 when Widnes had won the Championship and I was immediately impressed with his style and approach to playing the game. He seemed to glide amongst defenders and always seemed to be in the right place at the right time. To say that I was excited about playing for him is an understatement. Ellery had a very professional manner about him and his demeanour demanded respect. He certainly wasn't a disciplinarian in terms of shouting and bawling, but he would simply give precise instructions as to what he wanted done by the players. I cannot remember a single session during pre-season of 1999 when things didn't go the way he wanted. As a character, he was very warm to the younger players including myself and on no occasion did I hear anything negative from him. Whether he was a little more negative with the older players, I'm not so sure, but he certainly made me and the other new additions from the junior ranks feel part of the team. People talk about sporting greats having a certain aura surrounding them, and although I was still only a young man when I began training with the first team, I was in awe of him. He had the great ability to remain calm when everybody else was panicking and he had a calming influence over individuals that were having a bit of a nightmare on the field.

Not that Saints had been given many nightmares during the 1999 season, when they had won the Super League title, but as with every sporting team, you have your good days and your bad days. Unbeknown to us, a bad day wasn't so far off. Winning the Grand Final the previous season meant that the new season begins with the World Club Challenge against the Australian champions. Being given a squad number at the beginning of 2000 was one of the proudest moments of my time as a rugby player and in my mind it was a reward for the effort I had put in during the pre-season training programme. I felt that the coaching staff had rewarded me with the squad number and they must have seen me as part of their plans for the coming season, even though I was awarded one of the later numbers of the squad, number 26. With the World Club Challenge in mind for the early part of 2000, training recommenced just after New Year, and from this point on I remember being thrown fully into the skills and game preparation stage of pre-season training.

Working out the team's game plans for the coming season was a major part of what we did in early January and although I wasn't involved an awful lot during the team run throughs, I was given enough opportunities to give me an appetite to challenge the other forwards. About a week before the World Club Challenge, intensity hit a new high and the training week became a lot shorter than I had been used to for the previous two months. Training normally began at either 10 or 11am depending on the response from the players to the previous day's session. If lads were a little leg weary, then we would be given an extra hour's recovery the following day. For me, it meant an extra hour in bed! Come to think of it, the Yorkshire lads always turned up on those 11am start sessions looking a little sleepy, and Ellery was travelling over at the time from Yorkshire with Paul Newlove and Kevin Iro. I do wonder whether the 11am starts were for the benefit of Paul Newlove, who'd mithered Ellery he was having to get out of bed too early. Anybody who knows Newy can probably tell a tale or two but I'll keep it short and spare him some blushes and just say that he always trained to his own programme with its own individual intensity! He was the best player in the team when I joined the first-team squad but he wasn't exactly one of the greatest trainers. He almost had an appearance that said 'I couldn't give a monkeys', but we all knew different, and when Newy played, he certainly turned it on.

Everything game related was cranked up a notch and, as the week wore on, the sessions were eventually cut down to just thirty to forty minutes. To the non-schooled, this may sound like a lack of preparation, but I can assure you that the intensity was like nothing I had experienced before. When we had finally arrived at our last session of the week prior to the game, we would normally have a team meeting. We would be called from the changing rooms and into the old bar and snooker room at Knowsley Road where we would be confronted with a specifically structured seating plan. The chairs would be lined up in rows facing up front so that the attention was all on the coach. The lads would be playing around, laughing, joking, farting, until Ellery walked in and there would be a deathly silence. It was time to focus when he came into the room. It wasn't through fear that we all gave him our full attention, it was because we knew that what he was going to say would mean something to us. It wasn't normally a profound speech, but just a few simple words to focus the mind. In my own mind, it was tremendously enticing and was like beginning a new adventure into the unknown.

On that particular morning, I remember sitting right at the back. My own thought process was that if I wasn't going to be selected, which I wasn't given the fact I was squad number 26, then I didn't want to be having selected players behind me. That might seem a funny thing to have in your mind, but it was out of the respect for my teammates. I was part of the squad, but I felt that the focus should be all on the selected seventeen. Ellery, starting at fullback, began to name the team for the game. Unlike other coaches I worked under during my time as a player, Ellery had a very personal way of naming the team. He didn't call a player by surname, but by christian name. I thought it was a nice touch. So the team announcement continued and was so far the team that everybody had predicted. I'd not made the starting line-up. I never expected to make the bench either. There were some very talented players that hadn't made the starting line up so they must be on the bench, right? Wrong. When there was only one name to be placed on the bench and my name was announced, I can honestly say I nearly passed out. I remember becoming very hot all of a sudden and when a few of the lads began to turn around and look at my reaction, it only added to the embarrassment. I suppose that I didn't feel I was good enough to deprive an established player of their spot in the team, but I must have been doing enough to impress the man that made the calls, Ellery.

I was incredibly pleased for obvious reasons, but I was also very, very shocked and nervous and the prospect that lay ahead. We were all aware of the facts surrounding the game such as the venue, which was JJB Stadium, the home of Wigan Warriors. We were also aware of the opponent. Melbourne Storm had dominated the NRL table the previous season and were a daunting prospect of an opponent. I had obviously never played at a level anywhere near the one that I was about to be thrust into, but once I got home and sat down to recover from the shock, the nervousness began to turn into excitement.

I called everybody I knew and gave them the news. A large majority didn't believe me and never actually believed me, so they tell me, until I walked out onto the JJB pitch. I would like to say that I remember everything from the team announcement meeting, to the final whistle, but I cannot. It has been over eleven years since the day of that game, and I barely remember a thing. I'd imagine the feelings I have already described were largely present for days after the game. The result of the game wasn't a good one and we were well and truly beaten by a much better Melbourne team, and I'm pretty certain that at the time there was bound to be a large degree of disappointment from the rest of the players and of course the fans, directors and those involved in British Rugby League. For me, although we had lost, I felt very honoured to have been a part of the game and I'm sure my family felt very proud I had been given a chance to show people what I was made of. It wasn't one of my stand-out performances by any means, but I felt that I held my own and that I wasn't disgraced. On big occasions like those, you expect your key players to lead from the front, and I certainly wasn't a key player during my full debut, but when I took to the field mid way through the second half, I made my tackles, volunteered to take the ball up and ran around for twenty minutes with incredible enthusiasm.

I'd like to think those qualities were a part of all of my performances from that point onwards, and although for the team it was back to the drawing board ready for the first league game of the season the following week, I felt strongly that the game I had played was just the start for my own career. Although the game hadn't gone to plan and the result was far from what everybody involved at Saints had expected, the general attitude amongst the players was to get out against Hull in the first league fixture and prove all the doubters wrong. I was surprised and elated in the week following the World Club Challenge loss that I was again picked on the bench. At the forefront of my mind was to take the chance that I had been given and to cement a spot in the 17. To do this I knew that I had to perform to my very best in every game that I was selected. I was quite a realistic young lad and I was never one to think too far down the line, I would simply look at impressing on a week-to-week basis. If I did that, then I was always confident Ellery would reward me.

However, things took an unexpected turn at the beginning of the league campaign. Completely out of the blue to me, Ellery was sacked. I'm sure there were some of the more established players that had an idea that the decision to part company with him was on the cards, but everything was new to me and I was just concentrating on my rugby. I was disappointed I wouldn't have the opportunity to play under Ellery a little longer, as I am sure I would have improved my game a lot under him. I got the feeling in those early days after his departure that it wasn't as much a shock to some people to see Ellery leave, as he had found himself in dispute with the board of directors the season before, having been suspended at one stage, and I think it got to a point where Ellery thought he wasn't the man in charge any more. Any head coach will tell you, that isn't the way things should be run.

As the days passed, rumours were rife and there were lots of established coaches being linked with the job at Saints, all coaches that were reputed to be very good. I remember hearing the name of Ian Millward during the first few days after Ellery's departure and, to be honest, I'd never heard of him. I'm sure that he'd never heard of me either by the way. But when he was appointed, there was a mixed reaction from the players as far as I could gather. It wasn't a lack of respect for 'Basil' that caused the mixed reaction; it was more a fear of the unknown and, looking back, I think it was the more established players that were nervous rather than the younger ones. A new coach was coming in to join a group of players that had already had success the previous season and amongst the team were players who commanded respect for what they had done in the game. As a relative unknown in Super League, having spent the beginning of his coaching career in England at local club

Leigh Centurions, the new man would no doubt ruffle a few feathers. I was actually very pleased we would be led by a man coming to the club to prove himself. I was in the same boat as a player, and I felt I might get a good run in the team early on if I could impress from the start.

Chapter 4

WITH THE ARRIVAL OF ANY NEW COACH at a club, there is a bedding in period where the coach would assess the abilities of the players within his squad. At Saints, the majority of the first-team squad were already household names and a large percentage were regular international players, so I'm sure Basil had a good idea of what he had at his disposal.

The first few weeks after his appointment were very much the same as what I had been used to under Ellery in terms of training times and venues, and also the content of the sessions. Basil pretty much took a back step, I guess in order to see the dynamics of the squad in action. He would have known about the abilities of the likes of Paul Sculthorpe, Sean Long and Tommy Martyn, who at that particular time were the men to make Saints tick. But I'd imagine he wouldn't have much of an idea where me, Jonkers, Bennett and Edmondson would fit in or, to some extent even Paul Wellens, who had broken into the first-team squad the previous season to us.

I was open minded with the arrival of Basil and I had a pretty good relationship with him from the start. Many of the lads would raise an eyebrow at some of the comments he would make from time to time. From what I can remember from those early days, he had quite a quirky personality, to say the least, and more than a few would have a wry smile at some of the activities we did within the training sessions, but I always felt that I was learning new skills and learning more about the game with every session. Once he had settled in properly at the club, he started to take a more hands on approach, and it felt like he was a breath of fresh air. We were doing things in training that were completely off the wall to me and things I'd never considered doing before. He had us catching tennis balls, dropping under poles held up by teammates before hitting tackle shields, and even working on our line speed holding hands!

We always had a little laugh to ourselves when we would begin warming up prior to any session on the field, and Basil would emerge from the changing rooms wearing his own training kit and proceed to warm himself up on the other side of the pitch. He would always be keen to join in any competitive game we played and was a regular during any touch and pass game, in which he would demand the ball at every opportunity to show us his array of passing and of course his kicking skills (on which he prided himself). One thing for sure about his first season in charge was that he kept me and the rest of the players thinking. Every day was something different and even when the weather was bad, and even though I wasn't always the keenest of trainers, I looked forward to driving to Knowsley Road.

The established players were learning, the younger players were learning and even Basil was probably learning new things about himself. That combination and the environment that was being created was a very healthy and enjoyable place to be and although there were days when he could be a bit cranky when there were balls being dropped, it was a great place for a young emerging player to be.

As the season progressed from those colder months of February and March, we were encouraged in training to keep the ball alive at every opportunity, and for myself, this was a big bonus as I had always thought I had a decent offload. The key to keeping the ball alive is that you have to have support to pass or offload the ball to a player in a better position than yourself. There was no danger of a lack of support from the rest of the Saints players. We had some of the most exciting players in the game at that time and whenever we kept the ball alive in training we looked extremely dangerous. Whenever we did the same thing in game situations, other teams couldn't get near us, and the pace at which we played simply couldn't be matched.

Defensively, although Basil never suggested this, it seemed to be a case of 'if you score five tries, we'll score six', although that didn't mean we were a team that totally neglected defence. I think it was just a matter of playing to your strengths and what would have been obvious to Basil when he arrived at the club was the skill levels of the players. It must have been an easy decision to make in terms of how he wanted us to play. I had already played a small part in the World Club Challenge before the arrival of our new coach and I was keen to maintain my place in the 17, so it was obviously very pleasing that I was given the chance by Basil to stake a claim for a place in his team. He had shown a lot of faith in me during his first few weeks at the club and I wanted to take the opportunity with both hands.

As the season moved on, things started progressing for me personally and my single appearance became two games, which became four games and, soon, we were half way through the season and at the top of the table, and me having played in every game so far. As a team we were getting quite some media attention for the style of rugby we were playing and although I wasn't one of the players who were being requested for interviews on a weekly basis, I got the odd call to speak about my own progress and that of the team. I like to think I was always modest about my progression, and I have never been one to blow my own trumpet, although during some of those early interviews I was obviously delighted inside I was beginning to make a name for myself, even if it was only locally amongst the Saints spectators.

One thing I did learn early on in my playing career is that you can't always please everybody or be a player that everybody rates as a good 'un, but I never set out to impress anybody other than my family. If people liked the way I played then great, but I never let any negative comments get to me. I always saw the positives in any situation. If I had a poor game one week, I would be working hard with extra training during the following week, and although I had become a part of the squad in 2000, I was still looking at chasing Chris Joynt for that starting back-row spot. I was always realistic enough to know that, at that point, Joynty had a lot of time left in the game and I respected that, but my own goal was always to dislodge him from the team or to take over from him once he had finished playing. I always thought this was a healthy attitude, to have the appetite to be better than one of the best back-rowers in the country, and it was that attitude that kept me going when I had one of my poorer games.

I'm sure there were times during 2000 when Basil analysed the team's performance and thought about taking me out of the team for a bit of protection, but I was happy in the knowledge that I was being looked after in a way that would make me a more rounded player, a more rounded person and a professional. The team was going great and as we neared the end of the regular season that year, with a possible Grand Final appearance on the horizon, it did become quite surreal at times. When we finished the season by getting to the Grand Final, it was a dream come true for me. I had played in the majority of the games in 2000 and I had improved as a player beyond all recognition. My season had started with a World Club Challenge appearance and it was to end with an appearance in a Super League Grand Final at Old Trafford.

Just like the World Club Challenge, there is very little I can remember about the build-up to the game, or the game itself. I do remember specific moments however that I was involved in and especially being a part of the final try which Tim Jonkers scored next to the right post. Time was nearly up on the clock and I had done my fair share of carries and tackles during my time on the field. I was in back play and with the scoreboard in favour of a Saints victory it was just a matter of time before we were lifting the trophy. Tommy Martyn was stood directly in front of me on the Wigan 40-metre line and we had a play-the-ball on the left touchline. Tommy turned to me and said 'make a name for yourself kid'. With that, he called for the ball and dropped me back inside. I was confronted by some tired defenders, including Wigan back-rower Mick Cassidy, and I somehow managed to make a break on pure instinct. As I approached Kris Radlinski at fullback and with that instinct in mind and the try line in sight, I tried to take him on to my left hand side. Being the defender he was, he put me into a position in which I would have to either take the tackle of pass to support. As I was about to take the tackle, our wing man Anthony Sullivan joined me on my right hand side and I gave him a flick pass that gave him the time to put the supporting Tim Jonkers away to score the try that sealed the Grand Final for us.

The celebrations of the try were fantastic and I don't think there was one of the lads that didn't jump on top of us. The conversion was kicked and the game was won.

It is moments like those I savour and memories that will live with me forever. I had been given a chance to play professional rugby league and I had taken the opportunity and done my very best with it. The after-match celebrations are not very vivid in my mind for reasons of alcohol consumption, but such feelings of jubilation I have not felt since that debut season.

It had been a long hard season both physically and mentally, and I was now in the mood for a long break. The season had certainly taken its toll, but I felt the hard work I had put in since my signing at seventeen had all paid off in a massive way. My bank account, although it wasn't filled with cash, was certainly in a better state than the same time the previous year when I was on just two thousand a year, and the Grand Final bonus of seven thousand pounds was the icing on the cake of a fantastic year for me.

A few days after the Grand Final victory, the squad had to attend an end-of-season review with Basil, who gave us all his appraisal, before telling us to get ourselves away from the club for six weeks and to enjoy our time off. Pre-season training was apparently just around the corner! I wasn't mentally in any fit state to even think about the first day of pre-season and so I took his advice and duly booked a holiday away with my girlfriend. The seven thousand pounds bonus obviously came in very handy and we enjoyed a very nice holiday that year in Gran Canaria. After the six weeks of lounging around, playing on computer game consoles and enjoying every weekend with friends in nightclubs, your body always tells you that it is time to get back into some physical activity, especially when you have been active every day for the best part of the past four years.

So when the time came to return to training, I felt

I was ready. I was wrong.

I had been drinking every weekend for six weeks, as any young lad at that age does, but for a now professional athlete it was a fantastic learning experience for me to turn up completely out of shape. And I can tell you that once you are, it takes you some effort to get back into some sort of condition. The pre season of the 2001 season was incredibly difficult and, as it was Ian Millward's first pre season with the squad, he was sure to lay down his marker and set some pretty high standards. Most pre-season training schedules that professional players do during November and December are very similar. Lots of running, lots of weights and lots of pain. That's the easiest way to describe it without being too technical. With Basil, we did lots of hill running and I remember that he used to shout about 'muscle memory' a lot back then, and most of the time it was when we were getting flogged and he was watching. Rather than taking his words on board, in my own mind I was just thinking about punching him in the face. It's funny when I look back but it certainly wasn't funny at the time.

The idea was that if you can programme your body and your mind to withstand the pressures put in front of you, then when the situation arrives and you face adversity on the pitch, which you inevitably will, you will have the experience to handle the situation and your muscles, including your mind, will have been programmed in the correct way. At the end of pre season and the beginning of 2001, and being the current Super League champions, we were again to appear in the World Club Challenge against the current NRL Premiers, the impressive Brisbane Broncos. Stars littered their team and they had players that could have graced any team in the world. So when we beat them on a freezing cold evening at the Reebok Stadium in Bolton, to say it was a surprise is a massive understatement. Following our heavy defeat to Melbourne Storm the previous year, we hadn't been given a hope by the bookies, and even our own fans, I'm sure, were pretty sceptical about our chances.

The Broncos players were in no doubt that we were there for the taking but we had different ideas that night. We had well and truly prepared for what we were about to face and we probably knew more about them that they knew about themselves. We hadn't done anything drastically different in our build-up to this game to our previous World Club Challenge appearance, but the thoroughness of our overall preparation with the use of video technology had a major impact on our performance that night.

One of the major bonuses for us on that particular night was the weather of course. The Aussies, coming from a summer climate and into the winter climate that we had just trained through for two months was always going to run in our favour, but I think the hailstorm on that evening came as quite a shock. I'll always remember the look on the faces of the likes of Tallis, Civoniceva, Webcke and Lockyer, they didn't know what was going on. Obviously we weren't going to hang around and explain, and we took full advantage to take the game by two points.

It was a fantastic victory for Saints and of course for British Rugby League and one that kick started another memorable season for the club and for me personally. At the beginning of the Super League season of 2001, I was very pleased to be awarded a new contract at Saints. I felt that my performances the previous season and the fact that I had cemented a spot in the regular 17 were worthy of reward and I duly signed a new deal for eighteen thousand pounds per year. The £500 appearance bonuses were also still in place. Although I knew that the majority of the team would be earning far more than I was as a basic contract, I was happy that potentially I could add a further two thousand pounds to my wage per month if I was playing regular rugby. As it happens, I was. I continued to be a regular in the team for both Super League fixtures and also throughout the Challenge Cup rounds and I was happy with the way things were progressing on the field.

I was also very content with my personal life and I was in the process of buying my first house with my partner Kerry, who I had met during March of 1999. Kerry, although not a rugby fan in every way, was very supportive of me during my early days as a full-time professional at Saints, and her influence kept me grounded during a time I could have well and truly embraced the life of a young professional sportsman. But, Kerry, the house purchase and my rugby kept me very focussed and driven towards my goals. We were a young couple, both working, and with a very good wage coming into our new property, and I certainly felt as high as I had been at any point in my life.

With every up, inevitably comes a down when you get a little ahead of yourself. Don't get me wrong, I hadn't become arrogant, but I think I may have become a little complacent with my own training rituals. The extras that had been a regular part of my training were becoming a little less frequent and although I never lost focus, I was beginning to feel I was undroppable from the team. I had performed really well for a while, but others had noticed a dip in my performance levels, none more so than the head coach. We were mid way through the season and we had made it through to the final of the Challenge Cup, which that year was to be played at Twickenham owing to the rebuild of regular venue Wembley Stadium. Our opponents were Bradford Bulls, who were a very dominant team at that particular time. The name Bulls summed up the size and power of their team very well, with the likes of Stuart Fielden, Joe Vagana, Paul Anderson and Brian McDermott leading them from the front row. I was obviously anticipating a very tough match. Throughout the week prior to the game I was doing my own homework on the players I was likely to be facing in the back row.

You can probably imagine my shock when Basil called me out of the changing rooms prior to naming the team for the final and explained he wasn't selecting me for the game. I felt like he had given me a kick in the guts. I was a young lad, and I don't think

I was particularly afraid of voicing my opinion at that age, but I remember just standing there without a word to say. I was immensely disappointed, but on the same token, I couldn't voice my opinion because of my shock. I just accepted the decision and walked away to wallow in self pity for a while. But I wasn't one to sit sulking in a corner, I was still part of the squad as 18th man and so I had to do my professional duty and dust myself down ready to help the players take on the Bulls. Incidentally, my spot in the team was taken by outside back Tony Stewart who never made an appearance from the bench that day, which made the decision that bit harder to take. I knew deep down I had made the decision easy for Basil due to my indifferent form leading up to the final, but I felt at the time that Basil didn't give me the honest reason for why I had been dropped. His explanation was that he wanted to run with Tony because he would be able to offer a bit more pace and versatility against the big boys from Bradford. Whether this was in fact the reason, I'm not so sure, but I trusted Basil and since then I have hoped that the reason was genuine.

We went on that day to beat the Bulls by 13 points to 6 in one of the worst spectacles of a final for many years, owing to the torrential rainstorm that hit during the game. The club were very pleased, as you would expect, to put another trophy in the cabinet, but as a non-playing squad member, even though I was a part of the travelling party to the game, the feelings just aren't the same when you don't put on your boots. With the heartache from the non-selection in mind, I made a personal pledge to myself that I would give it my all until the end of the Super League season. I felt I did and I offered the team a lot during the last few months, but it wasn't enough in 2001 for us to finish the season on a high. We never reached the Grand Final that year, which was a disappointment, but I could look back on the first two years of my playing career and say that I hadn't done bad at all.

On a personal note, there was still one positive left for me before the year ended. I was called by John Kear to say that I had made the Great Britain under-21s touring side that would be playing in South Africa the coming November. I was elated and very proud to have been chosen along with some of my Saints teammates in Mickey Higham, Mark Edmondson, Tim Jonkers and Mike Bennett as well as some of the players that can still be seen playing Super League on a weekly basis, players that have gone on to become household names and represent their country at the highest level such as Rob Burrow, Danny McGuire, Rob Purdham, Rob Parker, Ben Westwood and Chev Walker, to name but a few. I had never been out of the country before playing rugby league and I knew that it would be a great trip and one in which I would get the opportunity to play with some fantastic players of a similar age from other Super League clubs. Prior to leaving for South Africa and not long after moving into our new home, I was hit with another piece of news that would play a major part in the rest of my life. Kerry was pregnant.

Chapter 5

WITH THE NEWS OF KERRY'S PREGNANCY AT the forefront of my mind and with just a few weeks to go before my departure to South Africa for three weeks with the Great Britain 21s, we sat down and discussed the best way of moving forward regarding telling our parents the news. We decided that we would wait for a few weeks and give ourselves time to get used to the idea of the arrival of a baby. We took the decision that we would sit them all down when I got back from South Africa as the pregnancy was still in the early days and we didn't feel that we wanted to tempt fate. We knew that on my return, Kerry still wouldn't be showing any signs of being pregnant and so we felt it was best to leave it until then.

On the day of departure, we said our goodbyes, and I was off on the adventure of a lifetime. I'm not a person who takes anything for granted in life and I knew that opportunities to tour other countries only come around every so often and I had to make the most of the tour from both a rugby and from a cultural point of view. The aeroplane journey was set to be an epic with a flight of ten hours and we were all given sleeping tablets to knock us out for a few hours. I think mine may have been slightly stronger than those given to everybody else as I missed the majority of our time in the air due to a light sleep of eight hours. Arriving in South Africa was a fantastic experience and although my initial impressions of the country were that of shock at the sight of families living in metal huts along the road, the country grew on me for those first few days. We were greeted at the base by the staff and were made to feel very welcome.

I have described it as a 'base'. There is a specific reason for this. The actual place where we were located was known as The Farm Inn, and was nothing whatsoever like any hotel you will be used to unless you have stayed in a game reserve that regularly runs safaris to see the local lions and tigers! I couldn't say it wasn't exciting and I suppose if you are travelling to South Africa, or to any culture that you are not accustomed to, then the last place you want to stay is the Hilton. It was all about the experience for me and I'm sure the rest of the players felt the same. Well, perhaps there were a few that would have rather stayed at the Hilton.

We were greeted with open arms and welcomed into the South African culture. We were shown to our rooms (which we would spend little time in) and it was straight into one of two minibuses that had been given to us for the three weeks. The day of arrival, you could quite reasonably expect that there would be a little relaxation time, maybe a bite to eat before seeing the local sights, but we were on a Great Britain under-21 tour and that meant that we were there to do a job. The training facility we were using in South Africa was the home of one of the Super 12 teams as it was back in 2001, and was a fantastic facility, more than what I had been used to at Saints.

The rugby pitches were immaculate and the gym was equipped with some of the best apparatus I had ever seen. And believe me, we put it to some good use. If there were any players that were having any thoughts about us flying to South Africa for a holiday camp then the first day would have been a bit of a shock. Coming off the back of playing a full season back in the UK, a few were a little weary to say the least. The coaching staff, consisting of John Kear and Mike Gregory, were fantastic for us as a group of youngsters and they catered for our every need.

The management of the tour was without hitch and organised in precise measures. The fact that the players were battle hardened, and that both John and Mike were hungry to be successful made it easy when it came to producing performances against the South Africans. We played them twice, and in both games ran out comfortable winners. Some might say that the margins of victory, by 100 points and by 80 points were a bit of an embarrassment for the South Africans as the South African Rhinos team that we played was the full side and not an under-21s. It is worth mentioning that the majority of that touring team went on to play Super League and are doing so to this day and starring for their respective teams. You can only play against what is put out against you, as the saying goes.

My own tour had its fair share of ups and downs and, if I'm being completely truthful, wasn't as enjoyable as I would have hoped. Throughout the first few days of being in camp it was playing on my mind that I had left Kerry to deal with a tough situation back home and I was disappointed in myself that I had not persuaded her to tell our parents before I set off on tour. I had visions of her sat in front of her mum and dad at the dinner table over a Sunday roast and rushing off to the toilet with sickness. That'd take some explaining. But it was also the fact that I was only 21 and she was only 19 at the time, and I felt I should have been supporting her rather than be in a country ten hours away playing rugby. I know it was a fantastic honour to be selected, but it was a tough decision to make and one that certainly played a part in my own performances on tour.

The first few days' training went fine for me and we were working mainly on how we were going to play in the first Test match. Looking at game plans and different plays to catch the opposition out was something I was used to at Saints as a team that liked to attack, so I felt comfortable in what we were practising. But, three days into the trip, when I called home, I had a rude awakening. I had called to speak to Kerry who had been staying at her parents' house rather staying at our new house alone, and her mum answered the phone. I could tell by the tone of Kerry's mum's voice that things weren't quite right back home and when I enquired what was wrong, the inevitable line was given back. 'There's no need to worry'. Well there was. If you've ever been told that, then the first thing you do is worry. With my heart racing, and all sorts going through my head, my immediate concern was Kerry and the baby. Christine,

Kerry's mum assured me that there was no problem but that Kerry had been taken into hospital after collapsing in the house. In my mind, that was all I needed to know, and I was hurrying her up so that I could get to John Kear and tell him I was going home. Christine went on to explain that there was no major problem and that Kerry was fine. As you can imagine, on the tip of my tongue was the question 'and what about the baby?' but with a mother's instinct kicking in, she must have read my mind and said that Kerry had told her that she was pregnant.

From my end, there was a few moments pause before Christine went on to tell me that she was very pleased and that so was Mick, Kerry's dad. Kerry is actually the youngest of five, with four older brothers and, as you can probably imagine, her dad is quite protective over his daughter. I think my biggest fear was probably her dad finding out that she was pregnant, which had now happened. I remember thinking selfishly at the time that I was glad I was ten hours away! But, Mick was pleased as well as far as Christine said and I was just happy that Kerry and the baby were fine. She was going to be kept in hospital for a few days whilst the doctors ran some tests but they were confident that nobody had suffered any long-term effects. With that news, I asked her to pass on the message to Kerry that I would ring her in a few days.

With all this commotion in my personal life, the rugby preparation had been put to the side even though the first Test was only two days away. I had already spoken to John Kear about my circumstances and he decided to put me on the bench rather than throw me into the lion's den. My performance wasn't great in that game and as well as missing more tackles than I had missed all season back home, I came up with a handful of uncharacteristic handling errors that put the team under a bit of pressure. My preparation hadn't been great and, in all honesty, I shouldn't have played the game, but I wanted to get out there and win my first international cap as a Great Britain under-21 player. The victory in that first Test was emphatic and apart from an electrical storm mid way through the first half, the conditions were perfect for expansive rugby. We deserved our victory.

The week following the game was very much back to basics in terms of field work as we concentrated on keeping our core skills to a high level. Off the training field we were given free time to let our hair down and, although we all came from different club cultures, the lads adopted a Great Britain culture and stuck together in everything we did. There were trips out to steak houses, visits to the local shopping mall and even a day trip to Sun City where the gamblers amongst the squad lost quite a lot of money in the casinos.

It was on that trip to Sun City that quite a few of the squad became ill and the doctor had to use his full allocation of medication to get us all back on our feet. The journey back was one I will never forget, as the bus didn't have a workable toilet. We were also unable to stop the bus along the dirt tracks back to our base, due to the likelihood that we would be seen by the local robbers as a target. As we drove along the dirt tracks, it was pretty daunting to see young kids, maybe eight, nine, ten years of age, making bow and arrows. I was just happy to keep going at a pace and get back to the Farm Inn.

Once we arrived back, it was a sprint challenge amongst half a dozen of us to make it to the toilet. I then returned to my room only to be met half way by the team doctor. Apparently, I was one of the lads who had been hit hardest by this bout of illness and the other lads were able to jump on another bus that was taking them out for a drink in the local town. I, unfortunately, was given a bed in the doctor's room so that he could keep an eye on my progress. I was given a heavy dose of painkillers and sleeping tablets to help me get over sickness and it wasn't long before I was deep in sleep. The next thing I remember was being woken by a loud knock at the door. I had been asleep all night and it was now early morning. I got up and was greeted at the door by Mark Smith who I was rooming with, and he immediately told me that we had been robbed. My reaction was one of shock and I quickly raced over to my room to find my belongings no longer in the place I had put them. I checked the wardrobes, the drawers and the cupboards and I had been cleaned out. As far as I knew, Smithy was staying in the room so I couldn't get my head around the fact I had been robbed. What had actually happened was that the lads had all returned from their night out and continued having a drink, playing cards in the bar area. A few local men had also joined them and somehow they had managed to get the keys to a few of the rooms. I remember thinking at the time that it sounded very unusual, very much like an inside job. How would a group of three or four men with holdalls full of training gear get past the heavy security that was in place at the front of our base?

One positive from this whole situation was that I had kept my wallet with me and I had the forward thinking to carry all of my money with me that day. On the negative side, they cleaned me out of everything that I had taken over to South Africa. All of my GB training gear was gone, as well as my match shirts that had been presented to me. It pretty much left me borrowing clothes for two weeks. As you can imagine, at this point on the tour, I was getting pretty fed up, and I was looking forward to getting home to see Kerry. I had already had an unfortunate first week and the second Test wasn't something I was looking forward to. I was heavy legged and mentally fatigued after a long season for Saints, my personal life needed to be addressed as soon as possible, and I was walking around the middle of a game park wearing just my underwear! I looked forward to getting back to normality.

I'll always remember to this day the look on the faces of Kerry and my parents when I met them at Huddersfield to be brought back home to Widnes. I had nothing but a plastic carrier bag in my hand and

I was able to answer the question they were about to ask before they asked it. Don't ask!

Chapter 6

ARRIVING BACK HOME WAS A GREAT feeling and although my playing season had come to an end, and there was no pressure in that respect, I had plenty of other issues that needed to be sorted urgently.

Kerry was my main priority, making sure that she and the baby were fine. It's all well and good getting assurances over the telephone that your partner isn't in any medical danger but there is nothing else like the assurance from the person themselves. The 45-minute drive from Huddersfield to Widnes stuck in my mind. I was in the back seat of my parents' car with my pregnant girlfriend (my parents still didn't know) who had been taken into hospital a week and a half earlier. I didn't know whether my parents knew Kerry had been in hospital or whether somehow it had slipped out that Kerry was having my baby. The journey was awkward to say the least. I didn't know whether this was the right time to tell them the news or whether to wait until we arrived home. I couldn't really open up to Kerry as I didn't want my parents to overhear anything that could have been considered odd conversation. So with the odd glancing look between us both on the back seat and the occasional smile in each other's direction, I kept the conversation strictly tour related and gave them as much detail as possible in order to keep them interested for the full journey home. Getting to the doorstep of our house was a feeling of sheer relief for so many reasons and to finally get home after an eventful three weeks was one of the best feelings I'd had all season.

The agenda for the rest of the afternoon and evening had been set without even discussing it and immediately on putting the key into the lock and waving goodbye to my parents it was discussion and decision time on how and when I was going to let my own parents know the news. I had, in the two years previous, played in two World Club Challenges and a Super League Grand Final, but this was the most nervous I had ever been. I was running ideas in and out of my head, deciding on how it should be done and then changing my mind.

I needn't have worried though. The following day, I called around to see mum and dad alone (Kerry felt it best I break the news alone!) and went into the house with my usual greeting and received the same greeting in return. I walked through the living room and into the kitchen and without a rehearsal or a hint of nervousness I blurted out that 'I had something to tell you mum'. As with Kerry's mum and that motherly instinct, she had already guessed what I was going to tell her before I had decided exactly how I was going to say it. I hadn't finished breaking the news and she was already in hysterics, of which I now know was happiness. There were tears and hugs from mum and handshakes from dad and it was a great feeling and a massive relief they were happy they were going to be grandparents. Kerry was equally elated that my parents were pleased with the news and for both of us it was the beginning of a very happy period in our lives. We knew exactly where we were in our own lives, our lives as a couple, and our future in the short term. We were both only young but we felt very lucky and privileged at the prospects we faced.

The off-season during October and early December of 2001 gave us plenty of time and opportunities to begin to get our new property in order ready for the arrival of our baby the following May. I had been given special permission, as well as the other lads that toured South Africa to have an extra few weeks of recovery before we started back with the rest of the boys for pre-season training. As this would be my third pre-season training programme I was now accustomed to the expectations and standards that would be set for us from the start and, although we had missed the first couple of weeks of fitness training, I had been doing some work on my own to make sure I didn't come back into the squad too much out of shape. Pre-season training would inevitably been just as hard as those in previous years but the start of 2002 would be slightly different, we wouldn't be appearing in the World Club Challenge that I had become so used to.

This didn't mean Basil went any easier on us, in fact I think he actually cranked things up a notch and really worked us over to make sure that we would hit the start of Super League on the front foot. 2002 was another season that will go down in Saints history as 'eventful'. We managed to reach the Challenge Cup

Final after some epic battles along the way, and as Wembley Stadium was still under construction, the final was held up in Scotland at Murrayfield against bitter local rivals Wigan. I had now become a regular name within the Saints 17 and although my value to the Saints board of directors hadn't increased in terms of financial reward, I was earning some good money for a 22 year-old, due to my match appearances. Things were going well, I had a lot to look forward to and I was looking forward to being a part of a Challenge Cup Final after the previous year's disappointment of being dropped.

The week before the final, we were due to play away at Bradford Bulls in a regular Super League game. Owing to the fact that we had a massive game on the horizon, Ian Millward, who wasn't afraid to make controversial calls from time to time, decided he would pick a 'slightly' weakened team to make the trip over the Pennines. Within the seventeen-man squad that day was yours truly and, past that, I can't really remember any more regulars from the first-team squad making the trip. The result was predictable; the focus on the team selection before the game was predictable and the match reports were very much predictable. I understand exactly what was going through Basil's mind, and although many people didn't agree with the selection of the team, I'm sure the majority out there understood his reasoning.

However, the non selection of so many of the team that was to travel up to Scotland the following week didn't quite pan out as we all would have hoped. We went into the Cup Final as clear favourites and we failed to deliver in every aspect of the game. The conditions for playing the sort of game we were famous for were perfect. We had our strongest line-up available and preparation had been as good as it could have been. In my own mind, if we could have played anything like we had done in the big games of the past few years, then we would take the trophy home, but as with all local derbies, the script goes out of the window. Games at the highest level are often won by the smallest of margins, and it is all about taking the chances that you are presented with. Teams make mistakes under pressure but the team that makes the fewest and is able to capitalise on those made by the opponent is the team most likely to win. On that day, it proved to be the Wigan Warriors who were fantastic value for their pre-match odds. We never had any complaints on the day and I think we were content, although we were disappointed, that we had given our all but been beaten by the better side on the day. That's just the nature of professional sport.

All champions always seem to be able to pick themselves up off the floor and strive for better and that is certainly what was in all of our minds after the final disappointment. There were plenty of Super League games yet to play and our league form had been pretty good, although not outstanding. Basil was always one of those straight shooters and a person I always respected for his openness and his honesty. There were players that didn't particularly like his approach and would tend to stay out of his eye-line, especially during video sessions, but I was always of the opinion that he was being negative for the reason of pushing players to get better. It was this up-front approach that in my opinion worked for us players at that particular time and, under his guidance, we could never be written off.

We went on to finish the 2002 season with another appearance in a final, the Super League Grand Final again, my second in three years. There was however a small matter sandwiched somewhere in between the beginning and end of the 2002 season. The birth of my daughter. As any father will know, the single greatest day of a man's life is the birth of his first child. The anticipation of becoming a father is one of the feelings that cannot be explained without stirring up some real emotions.

Friday 10th May 2002 was the happiest day of my life. I had woken the previous morning about an hour before training was to begin at 10am, and I had breakfast as I normally would prior to leaving for training. Kerry was up also and was relaxing between a cup of tea and breakfast television. She was very heavily pregnant and in fact had gone over the due date by almost two weeks so, although we weren't particularly nervous, we both sort of knew that the new arrival was imminent. At this stage, we were still unaware of the sex of the baby as we wanted the whole experience to be as full of surprise as it possibly could be, and although the previous day Kerry had said she was feeling a little uncomfortable, and this particular morning she was feeling the same, neither of us felt it was time to go to hospital. So with kit bag in hand, I made my way to training and participated as normal. I had given my mobile phone to Stan Wall our kit man and had asked him to call me out of the session should he receive the call from Kerry. But no call came, and I finished the day's work just after 1pm and made my way home.

When I arrived home, Kerry was looking slightly more uncomfortable than when I left that morning, but there were no major concerns other than slight pain, which she now had become used to. The day continued uneventfully until about 5.30pm when Kerry decided enough was enough and that things had progressed to what she thought was contractions. Being a typical man, and especially a rugby-playing man with a tough-as-teak exterior, I kept my cool for the sake of Kerry. If I could have screamed and run down the street calling for help I would have done! We had enough time to pick Kerry's mum up along the way, even though it was in the opposite direction to the hospital. I was told that a girl needs her mum at times like this! We eventually arrived at the hospital and were taken into a delivery suite in which we sat until the early hours of the morning. Not being the most educated in terms of the delivery of babies, I expected the whole thing to be over a lot quicker. As a man, you are particularly helpless in these situations although you are more than useful at being shouted at for the smallest of things. But, I offered as much support I could and when my daughter, Sian, was finally born a good six-and-half hours after Kerry had arrived at hospital, the mix of emotions was immense. I remember holding her in my arms similar to the way that I had held a rugby ball the previous afternoon, but I suppose if you've had no practise, then it can't be perfect immediately can it? I quickly got the hang of it with some guidance, and I was pleased to announce to everybody I knew that I was a proud father of a lovely baby girl. I left Kerry and Sian to sleep off the early-morning struggles and set off for home at about half past six in the morning. On the way home, I left Basil a message with the good news and told him that I would be spending the morning in bed rather than running up hills at Sherdley Park, I don't think he had a problem with that. I arrived at home when it started to get light and remember thinking I couldn't wait to climb into bed after such a tiring night.

The next few days I visited Kerry and Sian at every opportunity as well as focussing at training on the upcoming game. Once Kerry was home from hospital with our daughter, it was back to business as usual at Saints and striving for a strong finish to the season. One of the many positives in our life at that time was my ability to be able to spoil our new daughter with pretty much anything that she needed. I can look back at photos of our after-match celebrations at the 2002 Grand Final and I have a few of me holding Sian on the field wearing a designer outfit costing £200. A proud father will do anything he can for his kids.

The final itself against Bradford Bulls was a

fantastic game and one that will go down in history for being such an even contest between two great entertaining teams. Old Trafford was a venue that brought together everything that was great about the game of rugby league. The atmosphere, the camaraderie, the colours, the noise, they all play their part in what is now the biggest rugby league date on the calendar. I was fortunate that this was my second. The game was quick and it was physical and both sides had the upper hand in spells throughout the game. The result finally went our way and by the smallest of margins, Sean Long dropping a goal with less than a minute to go, and the Saints had again become Super League Champions.

Whenever I have been asked in years gone by to recall the special moments of the games that I played in such as the Grand Finals, I always struggle to recall specific incidents, but I can always find memories from either before or after the whistle that will live with me forever, moments that only the players that played in the game can understand. Moments such as walking out to the cheers of 75,000 fans, celebrating a try, or lifting the trophy as a team. It's those moments that make the time special, not the money, accolades, or attention that go with it. Being part of a team is the best feeling in the world, especially when you have a common goal and the hard work you have all put in to get there is eventually rewarded.

So another season had come to a close and with the Super League trophy back in the cabinet at Knowsley Road, my baby girl safely tucked up in bed at home and me and Kerry off to another after-match celebration, things were looking pretty positive. Once the headache had worn off and the dust from the season had settled, I received a phone call from staff of the England A team. I had been selected as part of the touring party to visit the South Sea Islands. The full Great Britain squad had also been named and unfortunately, I was told, I had just missed out. I was therefore automatically selected for the England A squad. Although I hadn't exactly enjoyed my previous touring experience, I was quite excited about the prospect of visiting Tonga, Samoa and Fiji and it was another opportunity I didn't want to take for granted. I certainly didn't have my 'holiday hat' on, but nevertheless, this was an opportunity very few people in life ever get. I didn't feel compelled to pull out of the squad, put it that way.

We met as a group a week or so after the initial phone call and the itinerary was set. We would travel down to London as a squad and we would be facing the incoming New Zealand team in a warm-up fixture for their impending Test Series against Great Britain. We would then fly out the following morning on our own tour. I felt fresh and invigorated from the ending to the season and I had enjoyed the year so far more than any other, so I wanted to throw my all into the opportunity.

When the time came to travel down south, I felt I was in a good place both physically and mentally and I had a feeling that the game against New Zealand was going to be a good one for me. As it happens, I did play very well, although we were well beaten, and I was satisfied that I had impressed the coaching staff enough to earn a place within the touring party's first seventeen, at the very least for the first game. The conditions weren't great that night, and there was a lot of spilled possession, but I managed to work hard, make my tackles as well as roll my sleeves up and get my hands dirty.

My performance certainly didn't go unnoticed, and not long after the final whistle I was approached by Phil Clarke, who was Great Britain team manager at the time. He pulled myself and Chev Walker into a side room next to the changing rooms and told us how well we had both played. He went on to tell us that we would not be travelling with England A but would be joining up with the Great Britain squad as 'stand by' players, as there were a few injury concerns with the GB squad.

I'll be honest, I had mixed emotions. I had built my hopes up and was excited about going on tour but I was trying to think clearly about the predicament I was now in. I couldn't be disappointed that I was on 'stand by' for Great Britain could I? Phil went on to tell us we were to travel home, and then we would receive a phone call from somebody within the GB camp telling us where we had to get to, to join the squad. With that in mind, myself and Chev re-entered the changing rooms, got showered and left the ground with the squad and went back to our overnight hotel in London. The flight to the South Sea Islands was due to leave early the following morning, so before I retired to bed, I had to speak with our own tour manager Pat Cluskey. At the time, I had only known Pat a little, although I would go on later in my rugby career to work with him, and I spoke to him about my own arrangements for getting home. I assumed that he had known about me now not going on tour. He did know. But, the slight problem was that he was unaware of how I was supposed to be getting back home.

In all their infinite wisdom, the management had given me instructions to return home to Widnes rather than go on tour, but they hadn't arranged for me to get there. I was left with two choices. I had the option of ringing my dad who would drive five hours into London to pick me up and drive five hours back home, or I would catch two trains from London to Runcorn and then take a taxi home. Hardly good organisation from such a high-profile organisation.

Eventually, I decided I would take the train option as I didn't want to ask my dad to book a day off work. I had three holdalls of training gear that need to be carted onto a train for a two-and-a-half hour journey. Just before leaving for the station, I gave my good luck wishes to the rest of the lads, and I approached Pat for the last time to pick up my train fare. I assumed the RFL, the sport's governing body, would be paying me for my troubles, and would be giving me the money to return home. This wasn't the case. I had to withdraw money from my own bank account for the £90 train ride.

I felt very disappointed at the whole situation to be

honest and let down. Not only had I just been placed in an unprofessional situation by a professional organisation, I had also missed out on a five-thousand-pounds bonus I would have received if I had travelled with the touring party. The one positive was that should I make my full GB debut then it would mean a seven-and-a-half thousand bonus from my club.

With that in mind, I carried my holdalls full of training gear back home and sat anxiously waiting for the phone call. I sat anxiously waiting for the phone call for a few days, which turned into a week and then into a week and a half and, by this time, I was getting a little bit confused, to say the least. My England A teammates would be sat on a Fijian beach sipping cocktails in the sun whilst I had been sat next to the phone in my living room sipping tea. I thought enough was enough and I called my club coach Ian Millward. I explained what happened a week or so ago and he had thought that I was in the South Sea Islands! He didn't even know that I was on 'stand by' for the GB squad. He was angry in the only way that he can be angry; he had a uniqueness about his anger. I received a phone call from somebody within the GB camp to say that there had been some sort of mix up and that the person who was responsible for calling me had messed up. I accepted an apology for my shoddy treatment and asked about the next step. I was told that I should continue to train alone and that I should wait for a phone call to join up with the squad. The call never came!

I went from the elation of being picked as part

of an England touring team, to even more positive thoughts as a potential Great Britain cap, only to find myself doing my own fitness training alone on the public field where my rugby career had started in 1989 as a Widnes Tiger.

Chapter 7

MY DISAPPOINTMENT AT THE END OF 2002 was short lived, as Saints were again to contest the World Club Challenge, for the third time in four years. It was always an exciting prospect facing the Australian Champions, as we always went into the game as underdogs on both sides of the world. The media considered the English teams far inferior to our Aussie counterparts and if you consider the progress that was being made on the international scene then the pundits were probably justified in their opinions.

But for the game at club level, the recent past had seen the British teams come out on top more times than they had been beaten, and we went into the game thinking positive thoughts. We had the experience as a group of players of playing in a winning final and also a losing final, so we all knew the feelings that were at stake. The squad that contested the final in 2000 wasn't a lot different to the squad that was available in 2003, albeit for a few retirements, and we had a certain element of invincibility, seeing that we had begun to emerge as the team of the Super League era.

Preparation for the game wasn't as good as it had been for past fixtures, owing to a handful of players carrying injuries and that meant the likely team to take the field would be somewhat under strength. It was possible that instead of being able to rely on the experienced players who we had relied on in the past, the baton was likely to be passed to the younger, emerging talents to see if they could handle the pressure of the big stage. We were heavily beaten and, in some quarters, we were embarrassed by a very experienced and well-drilled side. Sydney Roosters had obviously prepared well for the game and it wasn't a lack of preparation that caused us the problems in the end, it was the simple matter that the Australian players were individually far superior to myself and my teammates. As with every loss, there is always a feeling that you could have done better, but on that particular evening, we were matched for everything we threw at them. We didn't freeze at the sight of them at all, we were just too slow to get going, and once we decided that we wouldn't mind joining in, the game was over and we were chasing shadows.

On a personal note, my own career was about to take another move in the positive direction. Having been initially selected amongst the touring team for the South Sea Islands trip and then called back to the North West on 'stand by' for the Great Britain squad, the board of directors at Saints decided I was now worthy of a fresh contract offer. As I was still under the age of 24, and therefore still in contract terms 'tied' to the club unless another club would be willing to pay a transfer fee, the board offered me what they considered to be a fair offer. I didn't particularly think that it was an offer that represented my growing reputation or my growing value within the game but I wasn't particularly in a position to negotiate the terms. It was a goodwill gesture from the board seeing as I still had two years left of my current contract, and they felt that throwing an extra six thousand pounds at me would keep me sweet. The offer on the table was for £24,000 basic with the five hundred pounds match appearance fee still included. The contract would still be due to expire at the end of 2004, but by that time I would be 24 years-old, and I hoped that by that time I would be a full GB international.

Most players playing in this era will tell you that they would be happy to sign for a club if they felt that the money paid was representative of their value to the team. I always felt at Saints, although I was a very happy player, that I was underpaid. As contract negotiations go, you are sworn by the privacy agreement in your contract terms and conditions, which basically means that you should not discuss how much you are getting paid with other players. The situation could turn into anarchy as you can imagine. However, it wasn't hard to get figures from fellow players when discussing contracts over lunch and some players would be more than happy to discuss what offer they had on the table. I was always one to keep my cards close to my chest, but when it came to deciding to accept or decline the club's offers, I always did a bit of digging with the other lads. I was always disappointed with the answers I was given by the players, as my teammates always seemed to be on more money than me. As I've said, money was never my motivation, but the problem was I wasn't being paid what I felt I was worth, and there were players within the squad less talented getting quite a bit more than me.

I was now in a position in my personal life where I had a mortgage and a family to look after and, as everybody knows, the career of a professional sportsman is only a short one. I needed to earn as much money out of the game as I possibly could in the short time I had. I ended up signing the contract in early 2003 and put it in the drawer to concentrate on the upcoming league season. The injury situation hadn't improved dramatically and we began the season with a deficit of front-rowers, which meant that Basil needed me to step up into the front row at times. I wasn't 100 per cent comfortable playing there any more, as I had tailored my own strengths in the previous three years to playing in the back row. I was more suited to the back row because of my agility and my general handling skills. In comparison to some of the front-rowers that were playing Super League at the time, I would be giving away a couple of inches of height and a few stones in weight to the majority of them.

Basil felt I could use my strengths as an advantage when playing in the front row, and avoid the big collisions by being a little smarter than the big fellas. It worked well for the team and our performances on the whole didn't suffer in the early rounds, so I thought I'd give it my best shot. It wasn't going to be forever so I knuckled down and got on with it. The biggest difference of playing around the ruck at Super League level was the obvious impact that the front-rowers take tackle after tackle. You are expected to put your body on the line for 80 minutes and when the ball is turned over, you are expected to trundle it back up the field into the front-rowers that you have just been trying to stop. If they get a roll on in play and they get over the top of your middle defenders then, eventually, the defending team is on the back foot. I can't remember being on the back foot too often when I was used as a front-rower, but what I lacked in size and strength I gained back tenfold in tenacity and determination.

When our front-rowers started to return from their injuries, I gradually made my way back in the second row and my more comfortable position, but it was an experience that I enjoyed, and I felt that I didn't let the team down when I was selected at prop. The season progressed through the early rounds and we were building some momentum as the back end of the season approached. One of the renowned strengths of the Saints side during this particular time was that we could play well enough to win the weekly games without ever hitting our full potential until the most important part of the season.

But that particular year was quite a disruptive season. The injuries that had been there at the start of the season had returned towards the back end and if we were to retain our Super League title we needed to have that element of luck. Unfortunately for us, our luck ran out on us as we travelled to the JJB Stadium for the Elimination semi-final against

Wigan where we were soundly beaten by a battle-hardened team.

It was a night I will never forget, a night that was the beginning of the end for me as a player. I was selected to start the game in the right second row, a position that I had begun to make my own after some consistent performances throughout the season. The game started as all Saints versus Wigan tussles generally do with a little tension in the air and nerves on edge. Around the twelve-minute mark, we were in possession on the Wigan 40-metre line and it was last tackle, so the relieving kick was on its way. The kick was fielded by Wigan and they proceeded to bring the ball out from their own ten-metre area.

As Wigan approached tackle three, they were approximately midfield on their own 30-metre line and I could see they were bringing the ball in my direction. I had retreated slightly late from the previous tackle and by the time I got to the referee, the ball had already been played and Wigan were on the move. I quickly spun at the line and sprinted forward as quickly as possible to take away the available space and I was confronted by the figure of Wigan's front row man Craig Smith. My positioning off the line wasn't ideal to make a front-on tackle but I did my best to adjust my position in order to hit him just below the ball with my right shoulder. As he was carrying the ball tucked under his right arm, I felt that if I hit him where I was planning to then I could quite easily dislodge the ball and the plan was to get close enough to 'drop and drive' under the ball.

The game of rugby league at the highest level is so quick that sometimes, on the field of play, you have to make split second decisions. Sometimes they are right and sometimes they are wrong. In this particular instance I felt I had made the right decision and I was confident that I wouldn't come off second best. The collision itself was pretty fierce and on coming into contact with Craig Smith I was immediately jolted back and onto the floor. My initial reaction was of embarrassment as the chorus of cheers roared out from the Wigan fans and it wasn't until a couple of seconds later I felt unbearable pain throughout my right shoulder, right arm and my neck. Immediately after the pain I felt sickness and dizziness and almost passed out.

Our physio Claire Mannion ran on to the field of play whilst play was ongoing to attend to me. When she eventually got to me through several players, she began questioning whether I felt it was serious enough to leave the field. I decided that it wasn't an injury that was going to force me off in an Elimination Semi-final. I have been asked many times since the incident occurred, why is it that I wanted to continue playing with such an obvious injury. As a professional rugby player you become hardened to the bumps and bruises that are part and parcel of contact sports and didn't want to let my teammates down and leave the field with what I thought then was a 'stinger'. There was also the small matter of a potential Grand Final should we have won that elimination game and I thought that If we were to win, then I didn't want to make an easy decision for the coach and give him the chance to drop a player that only played 12 minutes or so the previous week. So I decided to try and re-gather my senses and get back into the defensive line.

At this stage, the pain was awful and I was beginning to get pins and needles throughout my whole arm and even into the right side of my face. I continued playing for a further five minutes before signalling to the bench that I was unable to carry on. I was immediately taken into the doctor's room at the stadium where I was assessed by both our own doctor Simon Perrett and the Wigan doctor and I was given the simple advice that I was not to return to the field of play. I was given a sling to keep my arm stable and I was ushered onto the bench where I stayed for the remainder of the game.

The season had ended on a sour note yet again for me personally, and for the team. We didn't have enough on the night to get close to Wigan who won the game emphatically. I was disappointed with my own contribution within the game, but I also felt strongly that I could not have carried on with the injury. On leaving the stadium, I was met outside by my parents who were obviously as disappointed as I was at the result, but they were more disappointed that I had picked up the injury. There wasn't any particular concern shown at that time by any of us, but we proceeded to make a very sombre journey home.

With the game being played on TV, I was able to watch the game back when I got home. My initial reaction to the incident in which I was injured was one of anger at the challenge that had been made on me by my opponent. I felt that he had raised his knee into the tackle. The video replay also showed direct contact to my right shoulder from his knee and was graphic enough to show my head jolting back and into the hard surface. Although I was unhappy with the incident, it wasn't one of my immediate priorities, and I felt that it would be sorted in due course.

My priority was to sort out my shoulder with the physio. Claire had advised me to rest over the weekend and to take the pain killers that she had supplied me with, and to get myself to Knowsley Road on the Monday morning for an assessment. As the weekend progressed, I was finding mobility increasingly difficult and by Sunday evening I had no use of my right arm whatsoever. I also had no feeling from the right side of my neck through my shoulder and down my arm to my fingertips, which meant that menial tasks were very difficult indeed. I didn't feel very positive at all about the results of the upcoming physio assessment.

I arrived to see Claire on the Monday morning and what I expected to be a long, drawn out assessment was anything but. On inspecting my arm, shoulder and neck, she said very little and immediately got on her mobile phone to speak to a consultant. I was obviously beginning to panic slightly at this stage, because being in the professional sport environment on a daily basis means you get to understand the injury process. It would often be the case that a player would be referred to a consultant if the injury required further expertise or even an operation, so when Claire got off her phone, I calmly asked her to explain what she thought was wrong. All she could tell me at this stage was that she felt there was sufficient damage in and around my shoulder joint to visit the club's shoulder consultant in Oswestry. This would be the first of many contacts and visits that we would have with Dr Simon Roberts.

Over the course of the next few weeks, we visited Dr Roberts numerous times to get a diagnosis and to prepare for an operation or a schedule of treatment and rehabilitation. I was given nerve conduction tests, physical examinations and scans on my shoulder and, eventually, after approximately a month, I was given some news I wasn't expecting. The doctor sat me down in his office and explained I had suffered severe nerve damage through my shoulder as a result of the impact of the collision and that the likelihood of me playing the game ever again was very slim. In fact he recommended there and then that I should retire from playing, as any more significant contact in that area could have far worse repercussions that could significantly impact on my everyday life.

I think complete shock is probably the only way to describe my feelings as I sat in the office after hearing that news. I didn't get emotional, I didn't shout and bawl, I didn't ask questions, I just sat and did nothing. I couldn't really take in what I had just been told.

I walked outside into the waiting room to be greeted by the physio and I told her what had been said.

She wasn't surprised. Discussing the options that I had on the way home in the car was an interesting conversation, as in my mind, the reality of what I had been told hadn't settled in and I was already thinking about beginning a rehab programme when I got back home. Claire advised me to have a sit down with my family and have a think about my options regarding what I could do after retirement, but her suggestions fell on deaf ears.

I was determined that the damning verdict given on my condition wouldn't see the end of me as a player. In fact, I couldn't let it be the end of me, because I had nothing else to do, and nothing else that I wanted to do.

Chapter 8

INJURIES NEVER COME AT A GOOD TIME, but this particular injury came at a time when things were again building momentum for me in my playing career. A week before the fateful game at the JJB Stadium, I had been named in the full Great Britain squad and it was obviously an honour and a very proud moment for me to finally get the opportunity to represent my country at the highest level. Unfortunately, the severity of the injury meant I had to withdraw from the squad.

After the diagnosis, I was pretty low. Just when things had been looking up again, it all came crashing down around me. I was, however, determined to return from the injury stronger and fitter than ever and, deep down, I probably didn't realise that the injury would see me out of the game a lot longer than I had originally thought. If I was summing up the injury details of my playing career up to this point, I would say that I had been very fortunate. The longest period I had been out of action had been a six-week lay-off with ankle ligament damage in 2002. I had reacted fairly well during this rehab period and I was determined to work hard with the physio to make sure that I returned from injury as quickly as possible.

Over the first few weeks after I had been diagnosed, I had given thoughts to what I would do if I didn't manage to come through the rehab programme and get back to fitness, and I didn't have a clue. I had never been anything other than a Rugby League player and other than a few part-time jobs, or jobs that I didn't see as careers, I was completely unprepared for the eventuality of finishing playing. Whether that was through this injury, an injury further down the line or the inevitable retirement in my early 30s, I had absolutely no idea what my interests were outside of the game. It was quite a scary place to be. I had no career planning mapped out and I didn't know which direction I would want to go in, and it was this fear that played a major part in my decision to commit to a rehab programme to try and regain my fitness.

I began my rehab programme at the beginning of November 2003, without really understanding what would be involved, and how long I would be answerable to the physio. I have always been a person that likes to see light at the end of the tunnel and it was important for me to know the worst-case scenario in terms of the length of the programme. I was very shocked to learn that for me to get anywhere near the levels of fitness I had been at prior to my injury, then I would be looking at a period out of the game of ten months. Rather than deter me from the hard work that lay ahead, It only made me more determined to return to playing earlier than that, but I knew that it would mean me making immense sacrifices of my time, and effort.

During the first few months of rehab, I was confined to the physio room with Claire and I had very little movement whatsoever in my arm, shoulder and hand. Gripping, lifting and moving exercises were very much the bulk of the exercises I would do, and you can only do so many of these exercises before they become mind numbing. My mental toughness as a person would be seriously put to the test at times but I knew that it would be a slow process and I had made a commitment to myself to give it everything I had in my power.

Progression and improvement was very slow and, at times, it was very lonely being separated from the squad of players that I had been used to training with on a daily basis for four years, but at Saints, we were likely a family, and I wasn't far from the thoughts of the players and staff, who would often nip over to the physio room and see how I was doing. As the months passed by, the improvements did start to progress a little quicker and, once I had a decent range of movement within the shoulder and arm, I began testing my ability out that little bit more. The days were very long and I would often arrive early in the morning before the rest of the squad. I would also more often than not, be the last player to leave the ground. My days in the middle months of rehab were still very basic and incorporated the gripping and lifting exercises that I had now become accustomed to, but there was also a very heavy volume of swimming thrown in for good measure. I was never particularly a strong swimmer prior to my injury but my injury schedule involved daily swims in the early morning and in the late afternoon. At first, it was a matter of becoming comfortable in the water, and the progress was again fairly slow in the first few weeks, but as with all new skills, the more you do them, the better you become. There was lots of technique involved within those sessions and it wasn't a matter of getting from one end of the pool to the other as quickly as possible. Claire made sure that I was doing things the correct way to improve my shoulder movement.

During mid March of 2004, I had to return to see Dr Roberts at Oswestry for his assessment on both my current condition and also my progress. His reaction was fairly positive, seeing as he had advised me that the shoulder would not improve. He had told me during one of the first appointments that I had severed nerves within my shoulder and that if they were likely to regenerate naturally, then there would be significant improvement both in muscle regeneration and also sensation. As it was currently, the muscles in my right shoulder had disappeared and I had no touch sensation throughout my shoulder and upper arm. But, I had full use of my forearm, and my grip was reasonably strong.

The biggest shock for the doctor I think was that I had a full range of movement within the shoulder joint, but without the strength or stability that the muscles would provide. He felt that I had made great progress but was still very uncomfortable with my choice to try and return to the game.

After another session of nerve conduction studies, the results pointed to the fact that the nerves were very unlikely to return to full working order and, in turn, the muscles would not regenerate. Dr Roberts sent me on my way with the clearest indication that I would be continuing to play at a high risk of further injury to myself and at the risk of damage that would stay with me for the rest of my life. That was obviously not something I wanted to hear, but I felt that I had come a long way the previous five months and that with a further period of extensive rehab, I could foresee further improvements.

As it was, my shoulder ability didn't improve all that dramatically over the final few months, and although I returned to full training earlier than expected, what I considered to be full training before the injury, was in fact not full training at all. I had to maintain the swimming programme that had been assigned to me by the physio, and I had to take things slowly when in contact sessions with the rest of the squad, but the area that I felt that I was falling further behind was the gym strength training. No matter how much I wanted to lift those heavy weights above my head and off my chest, they simply wouldn't budge. There were times when I managed to get the weight up, but then had to drop it onto the floor because I couldn't control the weight.

All things considered, in the back of my mind, I knew that I would never be the same player again physically but I felt that I could make up for my new deficiencies by being smart on the field and playing with my head rather than on adrenaline. The biggest change in me came not in the physical sense but on the mental side of things, and this wasn't something

I was ever conscious of when I was in training or out on the field during games. It wasn't until I look back on my time after I had become injured that I realise there were times on the field I was a hindrance to myself and to my teammates. I would shy away from tackles that I would have been regularly throwing myself into before the injury. I wasn't putting my hand up to run in the ball any more and I would only carry when there seemed to be nobody else around. I was afraid.

Fear can be both a positive and a negative in professional sport, and sometimes the fear drives your adrenaline and the results see you getting the best out of yourself in a given situation. But my fear was different. Subconsciously, I was afraid of getting injured again and having to re enter a rehab programme. I was afraid of letting down my teammates in a big game. I was afraid of the pain that was involved in the incident in which I was originally injured. I was afraid that I would have to call it a day.

I have no problems admitting that I was afraid, it takes honesty and guts to face reality, but the bottom line is that my fear was borne out of not being in control of my own destiny any more. I didn't have the physical condition in which to pursue my goals and, mentally, I had become fearful. When I returned to playing for the first team in late June of 2004, I had already featured for the reserves a couple of times to get my match fitness back up to a decent level and although I had been a stand out in those reserve games and I should have been relishing the chance to return to first-team action, I wasn't. When I was eventually selected in the seventeen, my return game would be at the JJB Stadium, the ground where my original injury had occurred nine months earlier.

I managed to get through the game without any further knocks to my shoulder, but rather than it being through luck, I was very protective of myself during that game. Don't get me wrong, I didn't shun the workload required of me, or my responsibilities when I was on the field, but I played it safe and I didn't test myself and the opponents as much as I would have done in previous games.

My performances overall towards the back end of the season in 2004 were nothing special, but the more I played, the more my confidence grew. There were glimpses within some of the games of me returning to some decent form, and I felt, as the season wore on, I was becoming more like my old self. My defence improved and I was making most of the tackles required of me. I was also putting my hand up to carry the ball, and I was making some good yards, without breaking the line. I felt that as play-off time approached I had enough of a chance as everybody else in the squad of making the team. The incentive of playing in another Grand Final was my main motivation and, as I had already missed the Challenge Cup Final victory earlier in the season, I felt that this was my time to get my hands on some silverware again.

When you have had some success as a player, you want more success, and it is this that makes all the sacrifice and pain worthwhile. Unfortunately, Basil didn't feel that my fitness levels and my overall performance warranted a place in the play-off games and, if I am being honest, there were players that were in better shape than me. I was disappointed, but then I would look back and see the progress I had made that season after being advised I would never play again.

The season ended disappointingly for the team as we were beaten in the play-offs, but I was very much looking forward to working hard in pre-season and building myself back up physically for the 2005 season. I was out of contract at the end of 2004, but it was something I thought was a formality. I had been at St Helens for such a long time I felt that I was part of the furniture, and I didn't see myself playing anywhere else. I had sat down with Basil and spoken at length about my future as a player and he assured me that I was a big part of his plans. He expected me to return to my old self and was confident that after a big pre-season I could once again be pushing for a spot within the Great Britain set up. I was now 24 years-old and effectively, I could leave the club if I so wished, for no transfer fee, but at the point of my first negotiation with the Chairman, this wasn't even something that I had given any thought. I felt strongly that my future lay at Saints, but I would expect to be paid what I felt I was worth. A point that I made during the negotiations was the fact that should I have not been injured the previous October, then I could have now been a full Great Britain international, in which case my value would have improved significantly.

The Chairman took a different view. He felt that even though I had been named in the GB squad prior to injury there was no guarantee I would have been given my first cap. Therefore, he felt justified that the offer on the table would be the same as the current contract I was tied to. He went on to explain that I had a lot to prove in the coming seasons in terms of getting my form back to where it was in 2003.

I felt that his offer was very insulting, that I was worth at least double the current figure of £24,000 and I felt strongly that I would stick to my guns and hold out for a much improved offer. The chairman wouldn't budge on that figure and so I approached Basil for some advice. I got the feeling he was slightly disappointed that the negotiations hadn't led to the signing of a deal, and he assured me he would speak with the board and try and get an improved offer. I still had two months of my current contract to run and I didn't feel it was an urgent situation to resolve, so I left it to them.

In the meantime, I had heard a few whispers that Widnes would be interested in speaking to me. They were a team that had some experience on board and the rumours surrounding the club were that a new head coach would be joining, as well as some current international players. I was obviously quite excited at the prospect of playing for my home-town club and although I didn't take any specific action, I did some enquiring of my own. I had heard that Wigan front-rower Terry O'Connor was likely to be one of the players joining Widnes, and it was his home-town club as well, I felt that this could be a good move for me. I contacted Terry and enquired as to whether he had heard anything regarding myself and Widnes and, during our chat, he confirmed that Widnes was indeed interested in me.

I never pursued the interest any further at that point and I let everything progress naturally whilst I took full advantage of the off season, spending my time at home with my family. After a week or so, I received an unexpected call from the Widnes Chief Executive who explained that Widnes was interested in getting my signature for the next two years, and that he would like to meet with me to discuss a po-tential deal. At that point, I wasn't in the business of wasting anybody's time, and I gave him clear instruc-tions that I had been offered a contract at St Helens that would probably be improved upon in the com-ing weeks. I didn't however give him any financial details of the offer that I had been made by Saints. He made it very clear to me in the telephone conversa-tion that I was high on their wanted list and they ex-pected me to be their first Great Britain international for quite some time. This flattery was nice to hear and, although I was secretly very excited about the thought of playing in front of my friends and family every other week, I kept my cards close to my chest.

It wasn't long into the conversation that the detail of Widnes's offer was the main talking point. As with all business men, they will try and sell you the benefits of their deal and lull you in before hitting you with the figures and to be honest, although I liked what was being said about what the club could offer, I wasn't particularly hopeful that the financial side of things would be that lucrative. Imagine my surprise then when I was given the figures of £52,000 basic, with £500 an appearance. That blew Saints' offer out of the water. I was very surprised and, although the CEO clearly wanted to discuss the offer further, I kept the rest of the conversation short and assured him I would be in touch once I had given the offer some thought.

Potentially, with match fees, I could earn approximately £70,000 if I could stay fit and manage to play in the majority of the games and, although money was never my motivation at any point in my career, this was an offer that I had to give some serious consideration to. After speaking with Widnes, I got back on the phone with St Helens and asked for a meeting with the Chairman regarding my contract offer. I felt I had been undervalued by Saints and my Widnes offer only went to prove my theory. On meeting with the Chairman, I gave him the instructions that I would be rejecting the contract offer from him and that I had been made a very good offer elsewhere. I didn't give financial details or even name the club that had given me the offer. The Chairman gave some thought to what I had told him and he returned immediately with an offer of £36,000. I told him that the offer on the table elsewhere was still higher and that, at this stage, I would be signing for the other club.

At that point I didn't feel that negotiations were progressing as I would have liked and I was about to leave the room. Just as I was about to get up from my chair, the Chairman made me a further offer, which was to match what was on the table with the other club. I sat back down and as shocked as I was from the Widnes offer, I was just as shocked that Saints could jump from £24,000 to £52,000 without feeling that they had tried to get me on the cheap. I felt very disheartened at what had happened within the boardroom at St Helens, as this wasn't the first time I felt that they had undervalued me or played games. I left the club that day feeling very confused and travelled home to Widnes where I would have to give the offers some serious thought.

Over the following few days, I let everything settle down, and I spoke with Kerry and my parents about the offers. Both of them said that the decision had to be mine and that I needed to feel comfortable at the club that I would be playing for. I felt strongly that I didn't like what had gone on at Saints, and that Widnes had been up front and honest enough to offer me what they thought I was worth at that time. They felt I could contribute to their aims and that my shoulder wouldn't hamper me in offering me a two-year deal. My decision was made, and I called the Widnes CEO to tell him that I would be signing for Widnes. I had reached a point in my career, when I felt I needed a new challenge. Things hadn't ended at Saints the way in which I would have liked, but I had enjoyed some fantastic years at Knowsley Road and I had made some great friends and played with some world class players. I had suffered a career-threatening injury, and I had been under paid in my opinion, but they had given me the chance to achieve so much as part of a fantastic team and a fantastic culture. I will always be grateful for the opportunity I was given but, ultimately, I had to look forward to what the future may bring and a fresh start at my home-town club, Widnes Vikings.

CHAPTER 9

I WAS WELL AWARE THAT SIGNING FOR Widnes from St Helens would be seen by many as a backwards move for me, but I felt that the move would be beneficial for my own game. I had played at Saints with many internationals and as the saying goes 'I was a small fish in a big pond'. I wasn't considered to be one of the better players, I know that, and I felt on signing for Widnes I could become an integral part of them becoming a major team in Super League.

Although Widnes is a world-recognised name in the sport, there had been very little success on the field since the days of Offiah, Davies, Sorensen and the Hulme brothers but the squad that was being put together seemed to me one that could push the Vikings up the table. A new coach had been appointed in Frank Endacott and his wealth of experience from New Zealand and from his time in England with Wigan Warriors would no doubt have a positive impact on the squad. The challenge was something I was relishing.

From the early months of pre-season training in the gym underneath the North Stand of the stadium that had been built on the old Naughton Park ground, I felt re-invigorated by the enthusiasm of everybody at the club. It was a fresh and exciting place to be and everybody seemed to have their own personal agenda for success in the coming season. This was my sixth pre-season as a professional player and I was now considered to be one of the more experienced players within the group, even though I had just turned 25. The squad was a mix of both youth and experience and with the likes of Terry O'Connor, Mick Cassidy and Gary Connolly bringing through the younger players I anticipated a season in which we would do a lot better than people expected.

My own pre-season went very well and although it took me a bit of time to get into my stride after the previous 12 months of upset, I felt as strong and as quick as ever. My confidence was high and I was feeling very positive on a personal level about kicking onto the next level with my own performances. In the back of my mind, I still had some doubts about my shoulder and whether it would stand up to the collisions that would be coming my way, but having bulked up in the gym through November and December, I had given myself a bit more protection than I had had in previous seasons.

During January, I was given squad number 12, which was probably what people expected, but as a person, I am not one to take things for granted. Although I felt that I had trained hard enough to be awarded a starting jersey, there was always that doubt in my mind that I would be used as an impact player from the bench, as I had been for so long for Saints. I suppose there was a lot of expectation on my shoulders, having played for one of the best teams in the competition for the past five years.

In my personal life, Kerry and me had decided

we were outgrowing our first house and we were on the market for a bigger property. Sian was getting bigger, as was her toy collection, and our two bedroom semi-detached didn't give us the space we needed. We came across a property that matched our requirements on a new-build estate in Widnes not far from the Widnes ground and the area was ideal for a young family. The property was one of the last available on the estate, and so we managed to get it at a discount. I had signed a very good deal at Widnes and with no thoughts about retiring anytime soon, we felt we would put my wage to good use and into property. I was at a fresh starting point in my life and although things were hectic, with a young family, a house move and a change of club, I always remained positive that the decisions I was making would be sound for the future.

The beginning of 2005 wouldn't begin in the way I had become accustomed to during my time with St Helens - I wouldn't be involved in the World Club Challenge. However, this meant that we could concentrate fully on the beginning of the league campaign. We knew as a squad that a big challenge lay ahead, but pre-season training had gone very well and we probably couldn't have done things a whole lot different.

There were times during the season we showed some scintillating stuff and there were times when we were absolutely terrible, but on the whole, the performances were too average on a regular basis, and we couldn't compete at the level required consistently enough. It was a struggle at times and for a large part of the squad it was a feeling we hadn't had before. Myself and some of the older players had been involved in successful teams for the majority of our careers, and the losses that we regularly suffered were mentally tough to take. It's all well and good preparing in the right way but, when you get out onto the field and things start going wrong, it's then you need to dig yourself out of a hole. Unfortunately for us, and there was no lack of effort, we dug ourselves further and further into trouble in some of the games.

Inevitably, we found ourselves near the bottom of the table and, although I'm not sure we underachieved in the eyes of the bookies, we definitely underachieved when it came to the fans and ourselves. As the season came to a close, we found ourselves in a relegation dogfight, and it was something I had never experienced before. When you are near the top of the league, you still have the pressure on you to perform, but you feel invincible, and you feel like the teams below you have to challenge you. When you are at the foot of the table, you feel vulnerable and the things that you have been confident doing in the past, you now feel reluctant to do. It is this pressure that caused us problems in 2005.

There were too many players within the squad who were not used to competing at the highest level, and when your experienced players aren't at their best it's the younger player that you need to step up and be counted. The blame for relegation that season doesn't lie with anybody in particular, but with a combination of smaller instances and situations that when put together become important factors. The squad that was put together was talented enough to stay in Super League and the coaches and backroom staff did their best and, in usual circumstances, their best would have seen survival. The training schedule both in pre-season and throughout the season was as good as it had been at St Helens and we were given everything we needed in order to have a successful season. The bottom line is, simply, that when we went out onto the field, we didn't perform well enough. Whether it was a mental issue or a physical issue, I don't know, I can only speak for myself, but it was those on-field performances that ultimately cost Widnes their Super League place.

In terms of my own season, it started as good as any other season that I have had in the past. I felt physically ready for the challenges and that I could repay the faith shown in me and reach the expectations of me; to play well enough to bring international honours to Widnes. The problem was, with every game I played, I found it harder and harder to recover from the knocks I had taken. The games that were more physical than others would take me three to four days to pick myself up from. As the season progressed, the strength and stamina that I had built up through pre-season was diminishing week by week and I was feeling the strain of having to compensate for my shoulder injury by using other parts of my body during games. I found myself making uncharacteristic decisions and errors which put the team under enormous pressure and I didn't feel I was getting the best out of myself.

When I was 100 per cent fit I always gave 100 per cent, but in certain games, although I was giving 100 per cent, I was only half fit, and I felt that my body was being broken. My shoulder injury started becoming a major problem midway through the season and I was playing games having taken concoctions of different painkillers. I reached a point that season where I felt mentally broken and the fear that I had felt during the early months after coming back from injury had returned.

Mentally I was broken, as well as physically being in no condition to continue playing, and I decided to sit down with my parents for a heart to heart. My parents had been watching all of the games I had played since I started playing in 1989 and that was no different in 2005. They had seen some of my better performances and they had seen the worst performances, but this year they had seen me perform consistently below the high standards I set myself. They had originally been concerned about the injury but they trusted me to make the right decisions regarding my own health, so when I decided that I wanted to play on, they assumed that I was fit to continue. To keep them from worrying, I probably never painted an exact picture of the reality of the situation and, whilst at Widnes, I'm sure they had doubts about my ability to continue playing.

Towards the end of the season we were playing

Hull FC at home one Sunday afternoon, and the previous week's game had been a tough physical encounter. I had progressed through the week prior to playing Hull by trying to stay away from any contact work in training because I had been suffering with some neck pain, but I didn't want to let people down and felt there were people relying on me within the team, on the terraces and in my family. People were expecting me to lead from the front. I was selected to play in the game against Hull after declaring myself fit enough to play, as I felt that I had been in similar injury predicaments before and I had been mentally strong enough to push through the pain. This time it was different. During the warm up, and within a shield defence drill, I ran up to meet the tackle shield and, on contact, my head was jolted back. I felt a severe pain through my neck, shoulder and upper back, so much so that I had to go into the changing rooms to see the physio. Dan, the Widnes physio gave me some heavy treatment for almost 15 minutes to try and get me into some sort of shape to take the field, but the situation didn't improve. I had to withdraw from the game. I quickly dressed in the changing room next to the one the team were using, and I went upstairs to see my parents.

It was clear they were disappointed I had pulled out of the game and we chatted briefly before they left the stadium to go home. A ball hadn't even been passed. I was forced into a corner in which the only way out was to be up front and honest with myself. I couldn't continue any more. I wasn't as I once was and unfortunately the injury meant I had to make the most sensible decision and retire.

The day that I decided I was going to have to retire was a very difficult day for me on a personal level. I had managed to come to terms with the reality that I would no longer be a professional Rugby League player but I knew that it would also be a very hard thing to take for the people closest to me. Kerry had been supportive of every decision I had made since we had been together and as with all couples, if one of the couple is happy then generally that makes the other person happy. Kerry was comfortable that I was doing the right thing for the future.

I'd of course be lying if the topic of money never came up in our many conversations as, at times, we would discuss potential career avenues for me to go down. With a young daughter and another baby on the way, it was never going to be an easy decision. We knew that my retirement would put us under pressure, but we were confident that for the time being we would be able to take a bit of time to think of a pathway forward. My parents however would be a different story altogether and, as with the majority of parents who have children playing the game, they are emotionally attached to the game through you. Mine were no different to many others and would travel all over the country to watch me play. I knew that when I sat them down to explain the situation and effectively break the bad news that there were likely to be some tears and a bit of shock. The day that I went around to see them I was very nervous as to the reaction I might get. My parents had always been supportive but this would be a decision that would be likely to affect them as well as me.

I remember breaking down in the kitchen when I told my mum, and being immediately hugged by her with words of support. It felt like a massive weight had been lifted from my shoulders. I had felt under so much pressure. They both had their worries for me, Kerry, Sian and the soon-to-arrive baby, but they understood fully that I couldn't carry on in the pain that I was feeling. They understood that if I could have continued to play then I would, I'd have given anything to carry on, but they knew that the injury was beginning to have a major impact on my every-day life outside of the training and playing environ-ment. They knew I couldn't let that happen.

In the weeks and months following my retire-ment, I continued to work closely with the players at Widnes in any way I could. Trying to maintain a presence within the squad was important for me and, whilst the season was still ongoing, I felt that I owed a duty to the lads. I helped with the coaching of the reserve team towards the final few weeks of the season, whilst also trying to decide on a career after rugby.

It was a very difficult few months in that I didn't know where my future was either within or outside of rugby. I felt I had to somehow keep a connection to the game after an involvement that had lasted for the whole of my adult life up to this point and I think I needed that involvement in order to keep me sane. I needed to occupy my time as much as possible and I applied for countless jobs in many different industries without success. I suppose when you have no experience other than being a professional sportsman, and you have no hands-on experience of working within any other area, then you aren't really as valued as you like to think you are. With my playing credentials, I didn't really think I would struggle to find work, but three months down the line from announcing my retirement, there was still nothing bringing the money in. Kerry was due to give birth to our second child and effectively I didn't have a job and didn't see my chances improving anytime soon.

I had given plenty of thought to starting my own business, but I didn't know where to start and, although I had plenty of ideas, I didn't know which idea to pursue. By chance, the opportunity to work for myself came along. I was out on a night out with a few friends locally during September 2005 and I heard a rumour that there was a bar in the town that was for available for lease. At the time, I didn't give it much thought but the more I did a few days down the line, the more I liked the idea of running my own premises. I made some enquiries and decided this was something I wanted to pursue. The few weeks following the initial enquiry were very busy as I had a lot of things to put into place. I had to re-mortgage my house to the value of £255,000 in order to release the equity required for the purchase of the lease, as well as attending a course in order to get my premises licence. I was putting the wheels in motion and

I was committed to the project but I knew that there would be a lot of work ahead in order to get the bar ready for my planned open evening, Christmas Eve 2005.

When the formalities were eventually completed and the keys changed hands, it was a great relief to know I could now start building something of my own, for the future. Our new baby was due in the coming November and I had just agreed with Widnes that from November, I would move from the playing side to the coaching side and take charge of the Vikings reserve team. Things were starting to come together after a period in which I felt powerless.

Coaching had never been something I had really thought about, although I had built up a bit of experience during 2005 by helping out with the coaching at local under-9s team, Widnes Moorfield. I got a lot of enjoyment out of my interaction with the kids and I felt that I was adding some value to what they were trying to achieve. The most pleasing thing was seeing the improvement in the young lads in training and then watching them take their newly developed skills into game situations. When I was first approached regarding the reserves job at Widnes, I didn't immediately agree to the offer. Financially, it wasn't a lot of money on the table, eight thousand pound part time, but it was the opportunity to stay involved with the game at professional level that made me give it serious consideration. The club had been relegated, and I felt that I had played as much a part in that as everybody else involved, although there were some casualties within the playing and coaching staff that had been relieved of their duties. I eventually decided that I would accept the offer to join the coaching staff and I was confident I could help to improve the skills of the players and give the newly appointed head coach, Steve McCormack, more choice of quality players to choose from.

I was confident the coaching job wouldn't have a significant impact on the newly signed bar lease, and I felt comfortable that I could juggle the two roles as well as support Kerry through the latter stages of her pregnancy. It was bound to be a struggle but it was a matter of simply having to do it rather than wanting to. If I'd have had my way, I would have earned enough money through playing the game in order to feel comfortable enough to retire and take things easy, but as things worked out, I never made a penny of profit during my time as a player, and my wages were all spent on the bills; much the same as everybody else.

CHAPTER 10

WITH THE KEYS NOW IN MY POSSESSION, I set myself the deadline of opening the bar for Christmas 2005. I knew that it would entail long hours, as well as lots of physical work, and I wasn't exactly at the peak of physical perfection. I was still having major problems with my shoulder, which was affecting my everyday life and also my sleep, and for the general pain I was taking a lot of anti-inflammatory pills.

The purchase of the lease had been done fairly quickly once I had received the money from my re-mortgage and, with hindsight, I know that I didn't give enough scrutiny to the condition of the building or to the finances of the previous licensed premises that had been located within the building. Maybe I didn't give enough thought to the opportunity at the time, but to be quite honest, I was in a state of panic in my life and I was willing to give any opportunity that came my way my best shot.

During the first few days of occupation of the building, I was paid a visit by the local council's building regulations officer who informed me that the previous leaseholder had been running the bar when the building hadn't been fit for the purpose, and that he had broken the law by doing so. They assured me that for me to run a bar from this building was totally possible, but that I would have to have a detailed building survey performed. In my haste and panic to get the lease signed over to me, I had been that impatient, I had neglected the survey and I was now in a position which could seriously affect both the planned opening date and also my finances. I had set a strict budget for some internal cosmetic repairs and you can imagine my shock when the survey was complete and I was told the whole building needed strengthening in order to accommodate large amounts of people.

I had assumed that the building was fine as the previous tenant had run a bar from the premises but what the previous tenant failed to tell me was that he was doing so illegally and that he was being pursued at every opportunity by the local authority. I had made a massive error of judgement and in assuming that everything would run smoothly, I left myself in a predicament which meant I had to spend thousands of pounds strengthening floor joists in order to get it passed as safe. The building was a relatively old one, and whilst not in bad condition, there were other defects that were picked up by the inspectors. The fire escape staircase required some improvement and a full fire protection system had to be put in place. A fully working fire alarm system had to be installed and I was also told that windows had to be reinforced, as the bar was located on the first floor of a three-storey building.

The workload had become far greater than I ever thought it would be and now time was against me for the planned Christmas Eve opening. My budget had risen by almost £20,000, so you can only guess as to my mental state during the few months leading up to Christmas. With the help of a few friends, and my dad, I worked up to 14 hours a day to get the building ready. I wasn't bringing in a wage at this point, and although my final playing season at Widnes had given me the chance to earn some good money, the savings that I had built up in the bank were nearly all gone.

Despite the problems we were facing on a daily basis, I was always aware that my priority was the birth of my second child and making sure that Kerry was fine both physically and mentally. I had continued to work at the bar right up until the 13th November when my son was born. We hadn't known what sex the baby was likely to be and when he was born I was naturally delighted. My daughter was now three-and-a-half-years old and this was one of the happiest days of my life. Things weren't going well for us at that moment but the birth of Oliver gave us new hope and, as a family, something to look forward to. It only gave me more determination to get the work at the bar finished and ready for the opening and, for the next month, I worked my fingers to the bone. There were more setbacks along the way, but I felt I had no choice but to keep pushing through them and it wouldn't be long before we started to reap the rewards.

All the hard work we had put in, and the long hours and sacrifices that we had made, all became well worthwhile when I was given the approval to open up by the inspectors just a few days before

Christmas. I sensed there was a bit of anticipation from the public to see how I had turned the bar around, and our opening night was nothing short of fantastic. I invited all the players and staff to Bar Cocoa and although the heating wasn't up and running at that point, and there were a few teething problems on the night, the general consensus was that it had been an initial success. Trade from the general public over the Christmas and New Year period was very good and I met a lot of new people who enjoyed the atmosphere of the bar.

There was the occasional bit of trouble, but nothing that wasn't sorted out with a few quiet words. In fact, I very rarely had to throw anybody out for causing trouble. As well as taking control of the general running of the bar, I also had to fulfil my commitment to the reserve players at Widnes, and the opening few months of the bar coincided with the pre-season training programme for the lads. I also juggled my time at home with the family, but it meant that I was very tired and stressed most of the time.

Although the bar had been a success over the festive period, as with most customer-based businesses, you tend to struggle just after the New Year because people have spent all their money. The bar in the early part of 2006 wasn't making a lot of money, so much so that we started falling behind with the £1,300 mortgage payments and we again had to rely on my dwindling savings to make ends meet. The income at the bar wasn't enough to satisfy all of our outgoings at home, and it was starting to feel like everything was getting on top of me. The situation, as the year wore on, began putting strain on my relationship with Kerry and although we always ended up making up after the arguments, the arguments were becoming a lot more frequent. I was spending more and more time away from the family and not seeing the rewards financially for my time and efforts and, with a new baby at home I should have been at home a lot more than I was. I wanted to make a life for us as a family and I was determined I could turn the bar around. It wasn't just me that was suffering as a bar owner, the whole town had become quiet and people's spending habits were starting to change.

During the first quarter of 2006 I started to feel I had made a big mistake in acquiring the bar, as the income in comparison to my outlay was very much in the red. I had fallen behind with the rent for the lease, and I was also beginning to get letters regarding arrears on my own home. The rugby side of things at Widnes was probably the only thing that was keeping me from losing the plot and it was a very valuable outlet for me to vent my frustrations. In a way, the failure that I was having with the bar, and the problems that I was having at home brought out the best of me at the rugby, and I was able to not only see improvements in the players individually, but as a team, we were able to reach the Grand Final in my first season as a coach.

The success I was having was probably a key reason why I lost interest in the bar eventually and decided I would cut my losses. The profits had gone from two thousand pounds a week over the first few months of business to a measly sum of just over five hundred a week in the summer months and, although I knew trade would no doubt pick up towards Christmas 2006, I was stuck with a business that for ten months of the year would just manage to pay the wages of the staff, but not the lease on the building or my own mortgage.

I decided to return the keys to the building owner after giving the place my best shot, but I knew that I had to find something else to do and quickly. I considered the quick fixes, and the money-making schemes, I had a dabble at the bookies and seriously considered at times throwing some big money on the roulette machines. I was desperate to try and make some money so that my family would be looked after, but the more desperate I became, the worse decisions I made. I was getting further and further into debt with the use of credit cards and during late 2006, when we hit an all-time financial low, I was paying the mortgage by credit cards. In total, I had lost approximately £40,000 on the bar purchase and I had debts of more that £30,000 on credit cards. I had a quarter of a million pound house that was fully mortgaged and I had fallen nearly £8,000 behind on the payments for that mortgage. I was receiving red letter payment demands by the day, and I was getting myself further and further into trouble by looking for short cuts rather than confronting the problems head on.

Rugby was my outlet for my frustrations and my

family were the most important people in my life. I had two beautiful children and at no point did I ever come close to taking the easy way out and ending it all. That's not to say that I didn't have the thoughts about what would happen if…

I didn't feel I was in control of my own destiny. Everything I was trying to do to turn things around was having a negative effect and this was putting enormous strain on family life. I had been successful in my first season as a coach but my priority was trying to fix the cracks that had begun to appear in my relationship, which was showing the early signs of crumbling. Kerry had always been tremendously supportive of the decisions I made, because she knew that those decisions would be for the benefit of us all. I was never a selfish person, I don't believe, and I was never one for spending money frivolously when I had it. I would always give whatever I had to Kerry in order to make sure the children had everything they needed. As a player, my outgoings were relatively small, and although my money wasn't fantastic, I always found myself with money in my pocket. The kids never wanted for anything, and particularly when Sian was a baby, she had always had the very best of things that were available.

When you are no longer in a position of having that disposable income, it is very difficult to get out of the trap of buying expensive clothes and accessories and although you try to adjust your lifestyle accordingly, when you have a habit then, whatever that habit may be, it is difficult to break.

Chapter 11

THERE COULD BE NO ARGUMENT THAT MY injury and retirement had a major impact on every aspect of my life.

Christmas 2006 was a very difficult time indeed and, with hardly any money coming in and two young children who expected Christmas gifts, it wasn't the happiest of festive periods by any means, but as a family we managed to tough it out and make the best of a bad situation. The children were bought as many presents as we could afford and we showered them with as much fun and love as we could. The last thing we wanted was for our current struggles to affect the kids. After a quiet New Year, I got my first bit of positive news for a while when I was given a leg up by Geoff Burrow (Leeds and Great Britain scrum-half Rob's dad). I was given a job working within the sports department at the GMB Union in Wakefield and, whilst the travel wasn't exactly ideal, it came at just at the right time.

I was suffering through my own problems at this time, but my role in the position was to help amateur and professional boxers and rugby players get back into education and signpost them towards re-education. It was something that was both valuable and rewarding for me and I thought many times during my early weeks within that job there should have been a facility that had pointed me in the right direction during those early years as a young full-time player.

Maybe I wouldn't have been in my current situation if I would have had a trade, or maybe some university qualification to fall back on, but instead, as a young lad, I didn't exactly use my off time productively. I would often come home from training in the early afternoon and sit on the PlayStation for three or four hours until Kerry came home from work. Hindsight is a great tool for having regrets.

One thing that I certainly didn't regret was sitting down for a long chat, not long after my retirement, with Terry O'Connor, who I had played with at Widnes and played against many more times prior to joining Widnes. He had actually played in the fixture between St Helens and Wigan in 2003 when I had suffered my injury and although at the time I hadn't given any thoughts regarding the incident and any potential for compensation, it was Terry who persuaded me to pursue a case for damages against Craig Smith.

During the months after my retirement I took the decision to make tentative enquiries with sports lawyer Richard Cramer to see if I would be entitled to claim any loss of earnings for the incident which effectively ended my career. Those early meetings filled me with the hope that I might come out of any case with a positive outcome.

I'm not going to lie and say I took the decision in order to protect other players from injury in the future, it was purely a financial decision and one that I was more than comfortable with. I had been injured during the course of a game and although the incident itself was not penalised by the referee, I felt strongly that the actions of my opponent showed complete negligence for my own well being. I was a retired player at the age of 25 and I felt that I had my best years ahead of me if I had not been injured. Richard explained that the case would be very complex and would be a long, drawn out affair.

Other than the occasional contact in 2005 and 2006 with Richard and his colleague Oliver Marns, I left the case with them and trusted that they would give it their best shot for me. I had nothing at all to lose and everything to gain, but I was always aware that I was fairly desperate for a positive outcome to help me through the first few years of my retirement. Little did I know that after I had initially spoken with them I would endure some serious struggles not long after. It was welcome news then during early 2007 when I was informed the case had reached court and that both Richard and Oliver were very confident of a ruling in my favour.

I was desperate for money and desperate for a break of luck and this was my chance to get myself and my family back on its feet. Prior to the case reaching the courts, I was informed that Craig Smith's legal team had made an offer for an out-of-court settlement for one quarter of the figure I was claiming. Don't get me wrong, the figure I was claiming was quite substantial, and although the offer made was a large amount of money, I felt that they were merely testing the water to see if we were prepared to stay away from the courts. In my own mind, I wasn't particularly nervous about the prospect of going to court, but I felt that should they return with a new offer and, if it was more in the area I felt was acceptable, then I would accept it.

There was always the risk in my mind of going to court and the judge deciding either that there was no case for damages, or that there was a case for damages, but for a much lesser amount than I was asking. It was a risk I wasn't really prepared to take. Any amount of money would make a difference to us in one way or another and this was something I had to consider when we entered a stage of proceedings when there was counter offer after counter offer.

Around the same time that my life was being occupied by my court case, I had been working part time up in Wakefield with the GMB, as well as continuing my work with Widnes. It was whilst I was in this hectic period of my life that I received a phone call from the chairman at Doncaster Rugby League Club, Craig Harrison. It came out of the blue for me, as I had never met anybody from Doncaster. When I learned that he was calling me to see if I would be interested in taking control of the first team at the Dons, I was very flattered, to say the least. I was also inquisitive as to how he had decided that I may be the man for the job. I had been writing the occasional article for the weekly rugby paper League Express and Craig had managed to read a particular article in which I was talking about young British coaches not getting the opportunities of Australian coaches. I was of the opinion that fellow British coaches were crying out for the opportunities to prove themselves and I expressed concern that clubs were, and still are, very reluctant to take a chance.

He must have liked what he read. After speaking with Steve McCormack, who was the head coach at Widnes, about the conversation with Craig, I decided that I would meet with Craig, Doncaster CEO Shane Miller and Director of Rugby Carl Hall. I drove over to the Keepmoat Stadium with no preconceived ideas of what to expect but I was very impressed with the enthusiasm and the vision from all three within the meeting. The stadium and also the training facilities were fantastic, and although the results so far that season hadn't gone very well, there was a talented group of young players that I felt just needed some structures putting in place to see them improve as a team. My thoughts and ideas obviously impressed the Doncaster directors and they offered me the job there and then. I didn't have any doubts in my own mind that I could do a job and so I accepted their offer of a full-time position as their head coach.

I knew the opportunity was one I couldn't turn down. The ambition that I had to be successful sometimes got the better of me and I had some radical ideas of where I wanted to take the club. The directors and the fans welcomed me with open arms and although I had a tough job in my first week in the position, which was to add some experience to the squad, I was excited about the remainder of the season.

My departure from Widnes was not something I

had planned, although I was getting results from the reserve team and helping some of the young players' progress, I felt I needed to be given more responsibility. I've mentioned before, I sort of fell into coaching out of necessity rather than pursuing the job myself, but in making the step up to coach, and after a season and a half, I felt that I wasn't testing myself or getting the most from my abilities. It was sad for me to be leaving my home-town club but, unfortunately, there wasn't the money there at that particular time that could have given me the opportunity to work with the first team full time and the club already had an assistant coach in place.

Joining Doncaster as head coach unfortunately meant I would have to leave my job with the GMB Union and whilst I had enjoyed helping the rugby and boxing communities across the North West, I never particularly had any ambitions to progress through the ranks of the union. I had always been a rugby lad and I knew that if the opportunity to work in a full-time environment emerged then I would take it. Being a father to a professional rugby player, my boss Geoff understood fully and wished me well for the future.

My future as a rugby coach seemed to be taking shape and finally I felt I was beginning to get my life back in order. The money still wasn't a patch on that which I had earned in my final season as a player, but I couldn't complain too much as I had a contract and a regular wage coming in, which helped enormously to ease the stress in my relationship at home. We still had major arrears with the mortgage and the credit card bills, although too high for my own liking, were beginning to be reduced ever so slightly. The one major area of my life that I felt needed resolving in order for us to move on, was the house. Realistically, I felt that in the short term, my wages were not going to improve, and although I was picking up about two thousand two hundred per month at Doncaster, my mortgage was still around thirteen hundred per month. I also had arrears of around £10,000 on the house and hefty credit card bills. This left us in a precarious situation. The bottom line was that we could no longer afford a house that was worth over two hundred and fifty thousand pounds. The decision to purchase the house in the first place was probably the wrong one, and we could have made less of a jump from our modest £120,000 semi detached, but purchasing a house for more than twice the value of the previous one shows I was in the mental state that didn't even consider I would be retiring just a year after the purchase.

We eventually concluded we would have to speak with the bank and discuss our options with them but, in my mind, the only option for us was to return the keys. The property market had slumped dramatically at that time and I knew that if we decided to hold on to the property and sell ourselves, then we would be unable to at the price that we owed the bank. I also knew that property was taking a very long time to sell and the longer we stayed in the house the more arguments we were going to have as a couple.

My final call to the bank after some serious negotiations was to inform them that I would be leaving the keys in an envelope just inside the door and, on putting down the phone, we finished moving the remainder of our property into our newly found two bedroom apartment. I felt that a big weight had been lifted off my shoulders when we finally left the house and, although a two bedroom apartment wasn't ideal for a young family, I thought it was only going to be a short-term measure and that we would soon be able to rent a more suitable house once everything had become more settled.

Travelling over to Doncaster three or four times a week was something I really enjoyed and I'm pretty sure that Kerry probably enjoyed me being out of the apartment and giving her more of the very little space that there was. The driving time of just over an hour and a half gave me plenty of time to think clear thoughts and it was my own space to think about how I would approach the challenge of keeping Doncaster in the division. I remember seeing the list of remaining fixtures and the league table during my first week in the job, and it was a daunting task, trying to get the team off the foot of the table from a deficit of ten points. It was also quite disheartening to see that the remaining eight fixtures were against the sides at the top end of the table and, with a squad of young players it didn't take long for the reality of the situation to sink in. I remember thinking to myself I must be mad to get myself into some of these positions.

It was bound to be a challenge like no other, but it was one I relished, and the style of rugby that we played surprised our own fans. I encouraged the players to throw the ball around at every opportunity because we had nothing to lose and I knew that the opponents we would be facing would probably expect to have it all their own way. As the season came to an end, we had certainly surprised a few teams, most notably Dewsbury, who we managed to beat at home by 50 points, a result which denied them a place in the play-offs. Unfortunately, the work that everybody put in was in vain, as the club was relegated, but I was very happy that I had given the job my all and the directors must have felt the same way, as I was offered a new contract for the following season.

Prior to the end of the season, I was contacted by Oliver Marns regarding my court case, and he informed me that the other side wanted to meet in Manchester to discuss, for a final time, an out-of-court settlement. It was clear from their persistence they felt uncomfortable in having to go to court and this gave me confidence. When the day of the meeting came in Manchester, I was excited at the prospect of having a lump sum of cash in my bank by the end of the day and I expected the deliberations on the amount to be paid to be over rather quickly. Eight hours in, and there was still a fair distance between what we were claiming and what they said was a true reflection of my losses, and as the day wore on, I was getting slightly jittery and getting the feeling that they may indeed be prepared to take things to court the following day.

Richard, Oliver and me convened in a side room for a meeting to discuss our next move and, when I went into the meeting, I had one figure in mind, and that was the full amount I was claiming.

I remember a statement that Richard made during the conversation and his words rang true with me being in the predicament that I was financially. He made it clear that he felt the offer on the table was as far as the other party was prepared to go without taking the case to court, and he advised me that going away from today with something was more important for me than going to court the following day and having the decision resting in the judge's hands. He felt the judge could just as easily rule in favour of Craig Smith and I would be left with nothing. We decided to push them one more time for a further five per cent and, after some heated negotiations, the deal was done and we all shook hands.

I was ecstatic to be leaving Manchester with a large sum of money that would make a huge difference to my family's life and although I was disappointed I did not get the full amount I was aiming for and felt I had lost through early retirement, I couldn't really complain after all the negatives that had happened in the past few years in my life. The money would mean that I could finally look at making some serious plans for the future and I was adamant that I wouldn't be throwing this cash into any off-the-wall venture or money-making scheme.

Once the money had cleared, my first priority was

to try and clear some of the debt that had been hanging over us for some time and, although I wanted to use the money to put some steps in place in order for our family to prosper, I had a duty to repay the money I had used during those difficult times. I negotiated with my creditors in order to settle as many debts as possible. The housing market in Britain had hit problems and I didn't feel that putting the remaining money down as a deposit on a house was the best option. So I consulted a relative who had his own financial company and property investment company and he agreed that bricks and mortar in this country wasn't the best place to invest. We already had a roof over our heads and although it wasn't spacious enough for us, we weren't in a position to get a mortgage on a property due to the recent repossession, so I felt it best that we would stay put for the time being and look to move into a rented house once our six-month lease on the apartment had expired. It was suggested to me by the relative that I should consider using the money I had left from my award to invest in a Spanish property, as so many people had been doing in recent years. While everybody around us was struggling, those in Spain were prospering and there was a property boom. I spoke to my dad at length about my options and the Spanish option appeared to be the better one.

After all, you can't lose money in property? The information that I presented to my dad was quite mouth-watering to say the least and with the potential for increasing property prices, it was an opportunity that my dad decided to get in on as well. Once our decision had been made, it was a matter of signing the paperwork to our new-build property in southern Spain, sitting back while it was built and then reaping the rewards from this Spanish property boom. This time things couldn't possibly go wrong.

Chapter 12

THE CONTRACT OFFER ON THE TABLE AT Doncaster at the end of the 2007 season was one I couldn't turn down at the time. I had really enjoyed the season just gone and the extra responsibility of being the man making decisions was something that brought out the best in me. I had worked under some fantastic coaches as a player and, now I was a head coach, I felt that I could mould my own future and my own coaching style. I had my own opinion on how I wanted my team to play the game and, with the right type of players, we could achieve some success.

I don't mind admitting that having the job of head coach at the age of 27 turned me into a bit of a control freak, and although I wasn't in charge of all the decisions that were being made, I needed to be in charge of every aspect of team affairs. I was a little naive to say the least and, at times, I was a little bit arrogant I suppose but I was very inexperienced as a coach at that time and although I felt that I knew best in most situations, there were situations I didn't handle very well.

I always had honest intentions with whatever job I did but at Doncaster I probably didn't handle the pressure as well as I did in more recent years. Meanwhile at my home-town club, things were looking a little shaky to say the least. The club had been forced to enter administration and the ownership and direction of the club was up in the air. I had always kept in regular contact with the friends I had made during my time at Widnes, and I had heard rumours that the club would be re-launched by some of the former directors. My conversations with my friends at Widnes were nothing more than out of concern for their jobs and, having been unemployed myself for a time after I retired, I knew the sort of pressure they would be under. Former head coach and friend Steve McCormack had left when the club entered administration and he had been considering taking up an assistant position at Hull KR in Super League. As the rumours gathered pace surrounding the club, and new potential owners began to emerge, I began to get the feeling the opportunity might be there for me to return to Widnes as head coach after the experience I had gained with Doncaster the previous year. I was still very happy to be at Doncaster and I hadn't given any thought to leaving the club until I heard from several of the potential new directors of Widnes that I should submit my CV as I had a real chance of getting the job should they take control of the club.

I didn't submit my CV. Although I wasn't being secretive in any way towards my bosses at Doncaster, I wasn't keeping them informed of the goings on over at Widnes because I didn't feel it was something that concerned them. After all, I didn't see myself leaving Doncaster at this stage. Everything went quiet for a few weeks following me signing my new contract and I was enjoying my time with the family during the off season and preparing my squad for the 2008 season, although I had still kept in contact with Steve McCormack, who I had previously worked closely with at Widnes. Steve informed me during the off season that he had been approached by Widnes to take his previous position as head coach after it emerged that the new owner was likely to be a local businessman, Steve O'Connor, whose family owned a very successful local haulage firm.

When Steve O'Connor was eventually confirmed as the new owner of Widnes Vikings, I was well into my preparations at Doncaster and I had already signed the majority of my squad for the coming season. The training venues had been booked and every session had been planned to the letter from the beginning of December through to the end of January, but I felt that I still wasn't fully in control of team affairs. I was happy in Doncaster but I wasn't content and although the travelling hadn't been an issue I began thinking that at this point of my life I would be better served in a position closer to home. I had not long before received the money from my loss of earnings claim and I had managed to sort out the majority of my debts. My kids were at an age that I wanted to spend as much time with them as possible, and being an hour and a half away from home for four days of the week had already caused me a problem earlier in the season that I didn't really want to repeat.

A few months earlier, and mid way through my job at Doncaster, my daughter Sian, who would have been five at the time, had fallen off the trampoline in the garden and landed on the concrete path, breaking her arm quite badly. As we were training that particular night, it had taken me over five hours from the initial phone call to me from Kerry to get home. I wanted to be with my little girl immediately, as any father would have. So when the opportunity to return to Widnes was put to me by Steve McCormack, it was a decision I had to give my full attention.

The opportunity was for me to take a position as full-time assistant coach within the first team squad, with a particular role as head coach of the JETS (Junior Elite Training Squad). My contract at Doncaster, with a value of £32,000, was a fantastic sum of money for a coach in the lowest division of the leagues, and I was very flattered that the directors felt I was worth that kind of money. Widnes's contract offer to the value of £28,000 was obviously less than the contract I had recently signed in South Yorkshire but I felt that the shortfall was something and nothing and that it would be a small sacrifice to make if it meant that I would be spending more time at home with my family, and also working within a few miles of home.

I never regretted my decision to leave Doncaster for Widnes and, to this day, I still don't regret the decision as I got an enormous amount from my experiences at the Dons. But I certainly regret the manner in which I resigned from the club. The inexperience that I had at that point as a man manager was reflected in my method of resignation. I had given lots of thought as to how I would break the news to those at Doncaster who had shown so much faith in me and I felt that my decision to leave would badly let them down and disappoint them. I knew that with the beginning of pre-season training just around the corner, my timing could have been a whole lot better.

It wasn't something that had been dragged out over a few weeks, but my thoughts about rejoining Widnes had started with just a little feeling of home sickness that escalated once I had given it some serious thought. I decided that the best way of handing in my resignation was to let them know by letter but on the afternoon I intended to hand over the letter personally, the directors were not at the club. I made the regrettable decision to post the letter under the door of the CEO's office and then without shame I left the building for the last time as head coach of Doncaster.

Looking back, it was a cowardly way to leave and I immediately regretted the method I had chosen, although, as I have said, I didn't regret the decision. I had admiration and respect for Craig, Shane and Carl, and I considered them to be friends and I think it was my relationship with them that made the decision to leave so difficult and one that I couldn't do face to face. Once I had left the club, I informed Steve McCormack I wanted to join Widnes again and I was all set to sign about a week later, when through the post came a letter to say that Doncaster wouldn't be releasing me from my contract and that they had heard that I would be signing for Widnes. The situation had spiralled into one that could have been resolved properly should I have handled my departure a bit better. But Doncaster were obviously bitter and disappointed I had left them and they weren't prepared to let me go that easily. They felt I should honour the contract with them, and although things like this are never resolved by the person in question returning to work for the company, they obviously felt they wanted their 'pound of flesh'.

My employment situation was up in the air again although I felt it was a formality that things would work themselves out in due course but the situation failed to be resolved as amicably as I would have preferred. In the end, I agreed to pay compensation to Doncaster for the timing of my resignation which left them to begin pre-season without a coach. I had sympathy for the club, players, fans and the directors for the position I had put them in but I felt that, at the end of the day, I had to be selfish and think of my family before anything else.

The compensation I ended up paying to Doncaster was, in the end, taken from my Widnes contract to the value of four thousand pounds and, although I didn't like to lose the money from my contract, I was happy to move on to the next chapter in my coaching career and my life.

I began my employment with Widnes during December of 2007 and Steve Mac was happy to let me take control of the majority of the skills sessions with the first-team squad. I began to really get stuck into my new role and although the responsibility of being a head coach wasn't there, I had been given different responsibilities, my main one being to oversee the improvement in core skills of the talented group of juniors that were on the fringes of the first-team squad. I felt that I added tremendous value to the players in working those extra sessions and I was able to not only advise them on the physical skills they needed but, having come through the academy and reserve systems at St Helens, I felt that I was the perfect person to mentally prepare them to become regular first-team players.

As well as delivery of sessions for both the JETS and the first-team squad, the move back to Widnes gave me the opportunity to learn new skills and one of my roles in order to help Steve give player feedback, was to 'tag and edit' games using the OPTA system. I was able to provide concise data in terms of individual player reports, as well as working on ways to improve team performance. I was certainly busy, but I was beginning to really get a feeling of fulfilment from my role. I felt I was certainly adding value to the club and that I was becoming an asset and once again I felt at home in the surroundings of my friends and family. There was no pressure on me directly to produce results and although this would mean I wouldn't get the praise that is linked with coaching a big win, it meant I could concentrate fully on the player development, which I believe is one of my major strengths as a coach. But, unbeknown to me when I accepted the additional responsibility of working with JETS, this small group of players would play a much more important part in the season than I imagined.

By the time the club had been re launched in December there was only a handful of players retained from the previous year and the problem that we faced was recruiting players of a standard that would see us be competitive in the coming season. The other clubs in the division had been recruiting their own squads for some months and the better players within the division had already been snapped up elsewhere. There were still a few players on the market that would no doubt do a great job for us, but as a group of coaches, we knew that we would have a tough job on our hands to achieve a play-off position come the following September. As the club had entered administration a few months earlier, we were also aware that we would have to begin the league season with a deficit of nine points and whilst we were confident we could recover the lost points sooner rather than later, it was just another blow to our play-off aspirations.

The squad was eventually made up of a little experience, but lots of youth, and what was obvious from the first session was that what we would lack in experience, we would get back in enthusiasm. The players all had a point to prove and they were hungry to prove themselves worthy of their squad numbers. The season itself saw us produce some fantastic performances and although, overall, our form was slightly inconsistent, we were able to finish fifth in the league table after wiping out the nine-point deduction in the first three league games. We had achieved our goal of achieving a play-off position and although we were beaten in the knockout stages at Halifax, we were proud as a group at how far we had come.

I am never one to be drawn in too much by the 'what ifs', but we knew that if we had started off the season on an even footing with the other teams, we could have in fact finished third in the table and given ourselves an easier route to the finals. As well as the league in 2008, we had participated in the Northern Rail Cup, and our group games at the beginning of the season had seen both good and poor performances. We had been drawn in the group with Leigh, Blackpool and Barrow, and although we knew it was going to be a tough group to qualify from, we expected to do so. Being beaten twice by Leigh within the group was an early disappointment but we were able to brush ourselves down and eventually qualify in second place which meant we would play the winners of one of the other groups in the competition. We were drawn at home to Sheffield Eagles and managed to beat them before going down in the quarter-finals to a very strong Celtic Crusaders side who ended up causing us a few more headaches throughout the league season. I think the reality about the season in 2008 was that we were always going to be up against it, and with the squad that had been hastily put together, we felt we had performed admirably and although we hadn't won anything, we felt confident we could build on 2008 and go into 2009 with the aim of winning the league and the Northern Rail Cup.

Chapter 13

TOWARDS THE END OF THE 2008 SEASON, the lease on our apartment was coming to an end and we were glad to be moving on and into a property that was fit for purpose. Sian was now six years-old, and Oliver was about to celebrate his second birthday, and we knew that the apartment wouldn't be the place to spend our time throughout the winter months. Living in Widnes was still our priority, as Sian was at school locally, and I was working within the town so, rather than move miles away, we decided to take a house not far from where we had previously lived. The location wasn't ideal, as it backed onto a dual carriageway, but the cul-de-sac out front meant that the kids could enjoy some time to play without the worry of traffic. The house also eased the pressure on myself and Kerry and I knew that she would be more comfortable in the new space rather than the cramped apartment.

Following the end of the season at Widnes, the coaching staff met to discuss the plans for the coming pre-season and I was made aware that it was going to be my job to take control of all rugby matters during November and December. The rugby World Cup was taking place in Australia and Steve Mac was in charge of the Scotland team which meant he would be spending some of the British winter down under. Conditioner Colin Robertson was also involved with World Cup duty as Ireland strength and conditioning coach. That left just myself and physio Joanne to put the players who were not in Australia through their paces and, although we knew it was likely to be disjointed at the sessions, I was confident I could do the job.

In the coaches' meeting we discussed every aspect of our own pre-season and everything was planned to the letter. I was very much looking forward to being in the position as acting head coach and, whilst I'm sure it was probably a worry for Steve to leave his team in somebody else's hands, I think he knew that they would be thoroughly prepared for the upcoming season.

In actual fact, the months of November and December were very successful indeed and the players themselves said that they had worked harder than they had done before. I wanted to repay the faith that both Steve and Colin had shown in me by getting the lads in the best physical condition I possibly could and, all the time, improve my own relationship with them. We spent a lot of time in the gym and out on the hills and I wanted to create an environment in which the players could work extremely hard, but also feel they were enjoying doing the work. I wanted to make them realise that for them to get the best out of themselves, then they had to be in peak physical condition, and I went about my job putting them through their paces at every opportunity.

I was in regular contact with Steve during that time and was constantly sending email reports over to Australia to keep him in the picture and, whilst he had his other priorities, he always maintained his professionalism when it came to managing the club from afar. On his return from Australia in December I think he was pleasantly surprised at the condition of the players and, whilst I hadn't had them all at my disposal, the general condition of them overall was very good. We knew we still had more hard work to do on the training field and, although the conditioning and strength sessions would become less of a priority, we had to up the ante in terms of getting them ready to play and looking at game plans and tactics. During the fitness sessions I had delivered through November, I had worked heavily on the players' skill levels and I was confident they would be able to go straight into the team sessions on Steve's return and, advising him of this, that's exactly what we did.

Steve spending time in Australia didn't have any impact on the physical condition of the players whatsoever but, I felt at the time and feel the same today, that if you lose that bond with your head coach, then results are affected. I didn't feel that it was my place to tell Steve this and I'm sure he knew that going to Australia for a month and a half would have a slight effect on his relationship with the squad, but I'm sure he felt confident that when he returned those relationships that are so important would be rejuvenated within a few weeks.

The early weeks of January were very much the same as any other weeks of the season and we all worked hard to prepare for the first challenge, which would be the Northern Rail Cup. The club knew how important it was that we won the final, as this would give us our chance to apply for a Super League franchise and get back into the top tier of the sport.

I don't think that there was anybody within the playing or coaching staff that thought we wouldn't qualify and our first game against Oldham was bound to be a tough encounter but one, especially being at home, we thought we could win hands down. Preparation for the game was excellent and, as I said, physically, the players were in great shape, but I had the feeling inside that the relationship between Steve and the players had become a little fragmented by his earlier absence. Nevertheless, I was never in any doubt about the result and I knew that we had enough talented players in the squad to see us through.

When the final whistle eventually sounded I think the whole stadium was in shock. We had been beaten by 22 points to 20, and this wasn't something I had seen coming. We had outscored them by four tries to two but they had won by taking their kicking opportunities and knocking over two points every time they were in kicking distance. Loz Wildbore had also been sent off early in the game which added extra pressure to the team, and in all honesty, we didn't deserve to win.

The reaction from the fans was one of disappointment and I knew after the whistle that the pressure would be on Steve to explain the result both in the media room and the boardroom. I knew the owners wouldn't be very happy at all and they would emphasise that the loss could ultimately cost us our qualification from the group and, further down the line, the opportunity to apply for Super League. So as you can see, there was a lot at stake.

Initially, after the game, there wasn't really much being said about the loss and, as a group of staff, it was business as usual. In this particular instance, the business was looking at the video and coming up with the reasons for the loss. Myself and Steve met early the morning after the game and went over to our offices under the North Stand in which we had our TV monitors and the video analysis equipment. We hadn't been in long, and I was preparing the equipment to evaluate the game when the CEO joined us in the office to request the attendance of Steve in the Stobart box to meet club chairman Steve O'Connor. Steve told me to carry on with the work, and that he wouldn't be long, so I just assumed that the meeting had been one that had been previously planned and that maybe Steve had turned his phone off to work and the CEO hadn't been able to contact him. Therefore he had come over to grab him by person.

I never thought for one minute that I would receive a phone call myself 45 minutes later to be summoned to the same box. My initial reaction was one of shock, but at no point did I have the feeling that I would be sacked. When I arrived at the box, I was greeted by Steve O'Connor but I was aware that Steve Mac wasn't in attendance. I was asked to sit down and give my opinions on why we had lost the game the previous evening. I proceeded to do so. When

I had finished my match analysis, I was informed by the chairman that the decision had been made, in the previous half an hour, to part company with Steve McCormack.

Whilst the announcement came as a shock, in the scheme of things, it was nothing of a surprise. We knew that the result wasn't great and there would be disappointment surrounding the club, but I was shocked that the decision had been made on the back of one disappointing result, especially as Steve had always seemed to have a decent working relationship with the chairman. Steve O'Connor had been the person to entice Steve McCormack back to the club.

Once I had rationalised the decision, I realised that it was a business decision rather than personal. There was so much at stake for 2009, having missed out on a Super League licence in 2008 and the defeat to Oldham was a loss that went a lot deeper than just this particular game.

During my meeting with the chairman, I was asked whether I would be prepared to take control of the first team for the time being and get the morale of the squad back up after the loss, as we had another important fixture to play against Gateshead the coming week. The picture that was painted to me that morning was that I would be in charge of team affairs for an undetermined period whilst the directors gave some thought as to the permanent head coach position.

I was told that in all likelihood, they would bring in an experienced coach who had worked within successful environments before, and who I could continue to learn under as an assistant. I was told by the chairman I was very much a part of his long-term plans for the club and he explained he felt a personal responsibility to protect me during a time when the future of the club needed to be in the hands of a proven head coach. I felt very comfortable with what I had been told and I understood that, as a Widnes lad, and living locally, and still being considered young to be a coach, then the pressure would be on me if they decided on me as a permanent replacement. In my own mind, I was more than happy to get the opportunity to impress in the short term and although I didn't formally put my CV into the club for the head coach's position, it was a job I would have loved to have kept in the long term. But I understood the predicament that the club was in and I felt that as long as I had a future at the club and the Chairman saw me as an eventual head coach then I couldn't be disappointed.

I left the stadium that day, not feeling at all nervous, but incredibly excited at the opportunity. My own approach to the fixtures in the next few weeks was slightly different to Steve Mac's in respect that I had sat down individually with all of the players and asked them to voice their own concerns at the previous week's performance. This particular personal approach gave some of the quieter players a voice and gave them a bit of self belief, which was badly needed, but one of the most important meeting that I had was with some of the senior players who hadn't been getting on as well as we all needed them to.

Both Mark Smith and James Webster were both integral parts of the team and with Mark being the team captain and James the main ball player within the team, it was obviously an area that I felt we needed to pull together. It was obvious to me that there was a clash in personalities and, although that was the only clash between them, their own stubborn streaks were beginning to have an effect on everybody else within the squad. I managed to find some common ground between them both and made them realise their importance within the group and with the help of some of the more experienced players such as Jim Gannon and Toa Kohe-Love, I felt I could certainly get them moving in the right direction on the field.

I have always been a big believer in getting together a group of players and moulding them into a team. To me, a team has to get along, and has to have a common goal with pathways in place in which to achieve that goal. Having a bunch of talented individuals that have no common ground is never a recipe for success.

The next two games saw that team and the teamwork kick in and the belief I had begun to see on the training field began to shine through in the games. I had encouraged the players to enjoy their rugby, and, with so many strike players amongst the squad, it was clearly a matter of letting them go out and express themselves. I tweaked a few things in terms of the game plans that were in place and added a few of my own plays and ideas to the mix and the hard work that we had all put in immediately after Steve McCormack's departure returned us two victories and a much better chance of qualifying from the group after the disappointing start.

I had been left to get on with the job by the chairman and although I didn't have much more contact with him during my time as head coach, I knew that the results must have been a relief to him. Our final game in the group stages would be a tough trip to Barrow and, at that particular time, they had brought together a tough group of players that were very difficult to beat up in Cumbria. Trips up that way are never the easiest in regular circumstances, but we went up there in week four of the Northern Rail Cup knowing that a defeat would put our qualifying hopes in serious jeopardy. We knew that if we were to be defeated by a heavy score then we would almost certainly be out of the competition, which would be a big negative for the club, so we knew exactly what was at stake and what was required of us.

The injury situation leading into the game had been challenging to say the least and, although we had managed to get some sessions in during the week of the game, there were a lot of players in and out of the physio room. Unfortunately, half-a-dozen key players didn't shrug those injuries off and we were left with no option but to pick half-a-dozen young players for this vital game.

The performance on that day was one of grit and determination and although we eventually went down by 12-4, we certainly didn't disgrace ourselves.

The game had been an ugly spectacle which had been spoiled by the weather and we simply didn't have the pack available on that day for a forward battle. However, the narrow loss and the other group game results going in our favour meant we qualified by the narrowest of margins. The goal of winning the Northern Rail Cup was still alive.

In the meantime, rumours had been surrounding the club about the appointment of a new head coach, and whilst it wasn't something I was concentrating on, it was interesting to hear some of the names that could possibly be brought into the club as my boss. I hadn't given up hope of being given the job permanently and I didn't feel that I had done my chances any harm at all by getting us through the group. As far as I was concerned, I felt that I was still in the position and I had to continue the work I had already done until I was told otherwise.

Following the defeat at Barrow, we were back on home soil for the Challenge Cup and as the draw had seen us paired with amateurs Saddleworth we expected to come through the game with a comfortable victory. The result was a positive one and we ended up winning by 80 points and although the fans were probably expecting such a result, I was very pleased in the manner of the victory. The performance had been thoroughly professional and we had been ruthless when in possession, something I felt would be important the following week in our first league game against Toulouse.

In the week following the Saddleworth game, I

was called up to the Stobart box again to meet the chairman to be told that the club had decided on the person to lead the club for the league season. I had been told just a month earlier by the chairman that the person appointed would likely be a big name and I should embrace any appointment as a positive one for my own coaching career.

When it was announced that Paul Cullen was the new head coach I was slightly surprised, although I wouldn't say that I was disappointed. I was asked by the chairman whether Paul was a person that I could work alongside and I confirmed I would look forward to meeting him and building a coaching relationship. I felt that Paul would more than likely bring a different approach and mentality to Widnes than my own and I knew that his experience in Super League with Warrington was something I could draw on for my own development.

I spoke to Paul on the telephone not long after my meeting with the chairman and our first conversation was a good, positive one. He felt I had done a good enough job for the past four weeks and that I should continue the preparations for the Toulouse game whilst he took a back seat, which would give him time to assess the club and how it was run. So I continued to work the team and get them ready for the game, and whether the final result was a result of the hard work of the previous month coming to fruition or it was a performance to impress the newly appointed coach I don't know, but what I can say is that the 70-0 victory live on Sky Sports was one of the best performances the Widnes fans had seen for some time. The fluency we played with on that night was fantastic. I felt that I had put my own mark on the team in just five weeks, a mark that I hoped would signal a strong league campaign.

Chapter 14

MY BRIEF TIME AS THE VIKINGS HEAD coach had come to an end and I resumed my position as assistant when Paul arrived. My time in charge had seen me take control of all rugby-related matters and I had been very happy with the responsibility that had been put upon me.

I knew that Paul would come into the club and look to put his own stamp on things and do things his own way, as any new coach does when he joins a new club. But what I didn't expect was to see the work that I had been doing, that had brought the players together as a team, be pushed to one side. I'm fairly certain that this wasn't done intentionally, but every man has his own methods of working and getting results and Paul, as head coach, was now the man making the decisions.

My taste for the responsibility had obviously given me the hunger to have a major say in the decision-making process, but Paul kept his feelings very close to his chest and at times I found it hard to engage with him about anything other than rugby. I felt he valued my opinions on players and the systems that were in place, although it was quite obvious that he didn't always agree with what I was saying. As the weeks progressed, I found myself having less and less involvement at training, and my 'hands on' time with the lads was diminishing. I had gone from planning my own sessions and delivering those sessions, to watching to make sure that players were making the lines on 'mapping drills' or getting back the ten metres on defensive shape drills. The job of refereeing games within sessions had also been thrust upon me and I felt that, as more time progressed, the more and more I was losing my own identity.

I no longer felt that I was enjoying going to training in a morning and the on-field results and performances weren't helping either. Results after Paul's arrival had been very mixed and the performances that were evident in the Northern Rail Cup and in the victory over Toulouse were nowhere to be seen. I felt that the players weren't enjoying themselves. The systems that Paul was trying to put into place were taking some time to grasp and I don't think that having three coaches in such a short space of time, with such different approaches, helped the players mentally. We had lost some games that we were in positions to win, and we had also lost games that we never looked like winning.

Deep down I had a niggling feeling that if I could have been allowed to continue as the head coach then maybe I could have carried on where I had left off. Whether that would have happened, I have no idea. Results could have been just the same under me as they had been under Paul, but I would have certainly made sure the players were enjoying training and playing.

My time at Widnes was becoming less and less enjoyable, losing so many games was obviously not very pleasing for the chairman. Everybody involved in Widnes Vikings, whether directly or indirectly, knew that Steve O'Connor had ploughed a hell of a lot of money into the club and we knew that, as a businessman, he would surely want to see a return of some sort. I remember specifically the away fixture to Batley Bulldogs around the mid-point of the season and at times in the game, we could have run away with it. But we were guilty of blowing some scoring opportunities and we eventually capitulated defensively, enabling Batley to take the victory away from us.

At the end of the game, I immediately went to the bus, as I wasn't particularly in the mood to have a conversation with anybody. I met Terry O'Connor outside who, in his role as director of rugby, was equally as disappointed as I was. We chatted about the game and Terry asked me my opinions on why the team weren't performing and I told him what I thought, as honestly as I possibly could. My simple answer was that I didn't feel the players were enjoying playing for Widnes at that particular time and as Terry would have known, being a former player himself, if you have somebody who isn't happy, then they don't tend to get the best out of themselves.

We continued our conversation and Terry proceeded to tell me that Steve O'Connor was fuming at the current results and performances and that he had decided the rugby side of the business would be going part time as he was not prepared to finance a group of players and staff that wasn't producing the goods.

At that particular time, I didn't feel that the impending announcement would have any impact on me as I had a full-time contract and I had been told by the chairman himself that I was a big part of the future of the club. However, stood next to the bus after the game, Terry had asked me what I would do if I had to go part time, and I had just replied with an off-the-wall comment that I supposed I would have to get a part-time job. To be honest, it wasn't even something I was taking seriously at that moment in time.

Early the following week, and from a few other staff members in and around the stadium, the rumours about 'part time' began to resurface, and I thought it might be best to speak with Terry again and also the CEO. The conversations with them both hinted that we would definitely be going part time and not in a matter of weeks, but in a matter of days. I felt strongly that the club couldn't simply half my hours and cut my wages in such a short space of time and with so little notice. I decided to seek advice about the situation that I could possibly be in further down the line and, having spoken with my union and with a few people with knowledge of employment law, I was advised to contact the chairman directly to voice my concerns. After all, I had a family that was relying on my wage, and I had been in the situation before when we had been short of money and I knew that the situation would again put a strain on us financially.

I tried without success to contact Steve personally

over a few days, by telephone, and in the end, I decided that I would send him an email. I got no reply to my concerns. I also put my concerns in writing to Terry O'Connor and Alex Bonney, the CEO, and whilst I did get a verbal response from them both, they were unsympathetic at the situation I would find myself in should I indeed be made to half my monthly income. I was told that everybody was 'in the same boat' and that the chairman was unhappy with his outgoings, and therefore the club had to cut costs.

I didn't like what was happening as a matter of principle, which is why I was so vocal in my concerns. On the training side of things, Paul had begun to make some changes to the training schedule in order to accommodate everybody within the squad and he felt it best that we would train on an evening throughout the summer, when it was light enough to have some outdoor sessions and also allow the part-time players to train with the full-time players. It was after one of these training sessions that I received a call from the club's CEO. It was approximately 9.30pm at night and I hadn't long got in from Wilmere Lane where we had been training that evening when I answered my phone to be told in the shortest possible way that my presence at the club was no longer required. I had effectively been sacked.

To say I was in shock would be the biggest understatement in the history of mankind. I asked the CEO to give me an explanation, and his simple answer was that the chairman had decided that if I wasn't prepared to go part time, then I no longer had a future at the club. One minute I was preparing myself for a long affiliation with Widnes as a coach and a future head coach on the back of the word of the chairman, and the next minute I was leaving the club for not agreeing to slash my hours and my pay in the space of 48 hours.

I was astonished and deeply disappointed at the way I had been treated and during the next few days I tried again without success to contact the chairman for an explanation of his decision. It had become crystal clear to me that my time at the club had come to an end. After a week or so, I had had a chance to settle down and think things through with a clear head and at the front of my mind was my wages. I didn't think that dragging the club through the courts in a case of unfair dismissal, although this is exactly what it was, was the right thing to do, and although I was hurt at the method used to get rid of me from the club, I felt that it would be best for my own coaching career if I left with dignity. I called the club office and enquired as to the situation with the outstanding wages of my contract and I was told that I would be paid the remaining three months in full.

I was happy at least that I wouldn't have to panic immediately about finding work. But, although there was no immediate urgency, I would be best served trying to find something as quickly as I could, to try and keep the pressure to a minimum, as the first signs had started to reappear that me and Kerry were having problems. The years after my retirement had been pretty turbulent to say the least and although we had some great times, we also had our fair share of problems. Moving house so often obviously put us both under enormous amounts of stress and add in the financial problems as well as a young family, then things were bound to boil over on occasion. We had lots of ups and downs and Kerry being a young mum and being confined to the house most days with a toddler wasn't exactly her idea of paradise. The kids were, at that moment in time, both sleeping in our bed, and I was forced onto the sofa for the majority of the time, which meant we gradually drifted apart.

It wasn't something I wanted, but eventually the strain told on our relationship and we split. It was an incredibly sad time for all of us but, with the children being the main priority, we both felt that the current environment wasn't a healthy one for the kids to be living in. Kerry and the kids moved out of the house and back to her mum's not long after my departure from Widnes and it wasn't something that I handled very well.

A month or so after my departure from Widnes, I was able to use a few of my contacts within the game and get on the coaching staff at rugby union side Rotherham Titans. With a new job, and plenty of travelling, I found that I could take my mind off my problems in my personal life and I threw myself into my work.

I have never been a big drinker or a person with any particular vices, and I think that my lack of interest in any of those things probably kept me from going off the edge. My life was again in dire straits, as I had become used to too many times for my own sanity, and my outlet for the pain that I was feeling was to put my all into the rugby. I knew that the kids would be fine, and I saw them at every opportunity but, looking back at those first few months after the separation, I could have seen them a lot more. It was my particular way of handling things, and seeing as the job at Rotherham was only part time, I was able to get a job at local high school, Bankfield, as a community coach, which gave me more opportunities to lose myself in work. My time at Bankfield was only a brief couple of months but it was something that I enjoyed and I felt I was adding value to what the teaching staff was trying to achieve. I was helping out within PE classes as well as running clubs both before and after school and it was very rewarding in terms of building relationships with the students.

I was comfortable within the educational environment and when I was approached to become a lecturer at Priestley College in Warrington, in November 2009, it was an opportunity I thought would give me the chance to become a fully qualified teacher, and the first position I had held that could lead to a long-term career. I knew that I had to throw everything into my non rugby job. As well as holding down my teaching roles, my other work priority was at Rotherham Titans. I had originally sent some CVs to rugby union clubs offering my services as a defensive coach or a skills coach and, at that particular time of the year, I knew that the rugby union season was about to begin. The rugby league season was coming to an end, and the reality was that I would struggle to get a job in rugby league in the months of August and September, which prompted my decision to approach the other code. I was confident I would be able to offer a good service to any potential club that showed an interest in me so it was very pleasing when I finally linked up with Rotherham head coach Craig West as backs coach.

I enjoyed my time at Rotherham a lot and, although it was a difficult challenge to learn the rules of a sport that I had never played or coached in before, it was a challenge I threw myself into. I had to again take a back seat in the decision-making process but my own role working with the backs was not too different to the work I had previously done in rugby league. The players were receptive and very bright and I was able to work with them on some quite complex plays. The standard of the players was pretty high and although the skill levels overall were definitely lower than their League counterparts, the strength element of the athletes at Rotherham was slightly better than that which I had been used to in my code.

Although I was happy with my time in union, I was hoping to return to rugby league and when the opportunity did eventually arise it came completely out of the blue. I had travelled down to Coventry with the Rotherham Titans squad ready for a Saturday afternoon game and my phone had been on silent for the team meeting on the morning of the match.

When I checked to see whether I had missed any calls, I had missed a call from a friend of mine, but the friend had left me a voicemail message. I listened to the message and my mate went on to tell me he had seen an advert in League Express and Rochdale Hornets were on the lookout for a new head coach.

I was instantly interested in the opportunity. Within five or so minutes, I had spoken to my friend and managed to get a contact number for the Rochdale office. I called that morning and expressed my interest in the position with the club secretary. She took my details down and told me that a club representative would be in touch. My prior engagement with the Rotherham lads would obviously be my priority that afternoon and, with that in mind, having lodged my interest in the Rochdale job, I turned my phone off until later that evening. Turning it back on, on the journey home from Coventry, I had received numerous missed calls and also a new voicemail message asking me to call Mike at Rochdale. As it was now pushing on later into the night, I thought it best to leave the return call until the next morning

CHAPTER 15

I DIDN'T KNOW AT THE TIME BUT THE person leaving the message was already known to me. Mike Banks had been employed by Widnes in 2008 and my relationship with him at that time was a good one. His role at Widnes was on the corporate side of the business rather than the rugby side and although he never had any prior rugby league knowledge, he must have heard good things about me in and around the office.

My reputation as a coach must have been a decent one locally as I was to learn that he was calling to speak to me to ask why I hadn't put in my CV and application for the vacant position at Hornets. I hadn't known that the job was available. As I explained to Mike, I had been out of League for five months and, although I had remained interested in goings on from a distance, I hadn't been buying much rugby league press of late. The particular job at Rochdale had been advertised for a month or so and I never had a clue. In fact, Mike had been trying in vain to contact me on an old mobile number of mine.

I agreed to meet Mike and a few of the Rochdale directors at some point during the next few days and, when I travelled up to Spotland, I expected the meeting to be nothing other than an initial chat about the position and whether I would be interested in submitting a late application. It soon became apparent that the meeting seemed to be more geared towards them offering me the job, and I was asked whether I felt I could get a team together in a short space of time. I was told that the club had parted company with the previous coaching staff only a few weeks earlier and it had left them with a problem - there were hardly any players available, which wasn't great seeing as a normal pre-season schedule would begin in early November. It was now the middle of October.

It was clear to me from early in the meeting that my recommendation had come from Mike Banks who was now in position at Hornets as CEO, and he had clearly seen the successful work I had done during my time at Widnes, which must have given him the confidence to approach me knowing I could get things moving forward in a positive way.

I felt it necessary during the meeting to give myself a proper introduction, as I obviously hadn't handed in an application and I wasn't too sure exactly how much the board of directors knew about me. I told them of my background and, whilst they were impressed, they wanted to hear more about what I could offer them for the coming season. I was confident I could get a squad of players together in a short amount of time and, in actual fact, unbeknown to them, I had already spoken to a handful after my first conversation with Mike a few days earlier. I had prepared myself for any questions that they were likely to ask and as the meeting went on, I was clear in my mind that, should they want me on board, I would be very happy to take the job.

At the end of the meeting, with formalities out of the way, I agreed that I would become the new head coach for the Hornets and, whilst the contract I was about to sign wasn't the greatest financially, the opportunity to put my own mark on a team and on a club was one that I would be a fool to turn down. I had gotten on very well with the directors I met that evening and felt that it would be a productive relationship.

So all that was to be done was to get together a squad capable of being competitive. The chairman, Mark Wynn, CEO Mike Banks, and fellow directors knew that that would be very tough as they were all in agreement that the best players would have more than likely signed elsewhere. The money available at Rochdale was based on win and loss bonuses and they knew, although it was all the club could afford, it would be difficult to entice players to the club without the guaranteed payments that almost all our competitors would be paying.

But, I was always confident that I could pick up some players that were looking for an opportunity to either impress after coming from reserve-grade teams, or prove the doubters wrong after leaving other Championship One sides. My instructions and the goals of the club were to simply be competitive during 2009 and for them that meant not coming bottom of the league. They stressed that achieving a play-off position would be a massive achievement and, whilst I don't think they really believed that could be done, I was determined I would have a team that not only was a play-off team, but one that was challenging for promotion.

I knew that there were talented players available and over the next few weeks I went about the job of offering terms and conditions to players I felt had the right attitude and the drive to want to come and play the game at Hornets. I set myself a target of having a group of 20 players signed to the club by the middle of November and I was pleased I was able to get this done without too much of a fuss.

Within the squad, were players of unknown quality to me, and no doubt to many of our fans, but I had always been of the opinion that it is important to have the right balance of characters within the squad to create that 'team' and it was always a priority of mine to firstly assess the person as a person rather than as a player. It's no good having a great player with an awful attitude because, more often than not, it is the attitude rather than the performance that comes back to bite you.

When training began at the end of November, I had managed to pull together a total of almost 30 players and although I knew that there would be a few who would probably not be at the standard I required, the size of the squad kept everybody on their toes. Training was excellent throughout pre-season and although we suffered the worst winter for quite some time, and it was fairly difficult getting through to Rochdale at times with the heavy snow, the attitude and application of the lads was first class and we regularly trained in conditions that normally would have seen a session cancelled.

I could sense, even back then, we would be in for a good season. The club was making very good progress in the short term and I was throwing everything I had into improving the players I had signed. I had introduced methods on and off the field that the majority of the players had never seen or used before and the ideas kept the players fresh, so that they would look forward to coming to training, which was important in building relationships within the squad.

I was in a position in which I had to gain the trust and respect of the lads and, although this was an important part of my role in the short term, I also had to assess each of the player's abilities and see where each of them would fit into the team and, ultimately, my plans.

We had arranged a tough set of friendly fixtures and in late January of 2010 we were to begin our Northern Rail Cup campaign. I knew realistically that we had very little chance of coming out of the friendlies and the Northern Rail Cup fixtures in February with many victories but I was disciplined enough to know that I had to persist with the experimenting of players in different positions in order for us to have a decent league season. My prediction of losses during January and February was in the end correct but, although we lost all of those early games, we fought admirably against some of the best teams in our own league and the one above. We didn't disgrace ourselves by any means and for me it was a massively valuable experience in which I was able to pigeon hole the players into their best positions.

Inevitably, there were early season casualties and players left the club who were either not good enough for the team that I was building or players with terrible attitudes. There was still a lot of work to do to get the team in order but I was pleased at how far we had come in such a short space of time. Unfortunately for me, I didn't have the pick of the best players from the start but this only meant I had to work harder to improve the players I did have. I was always on the lookout for anybody who I thought might add value to the squad and as the season progressed we continued to add players and also release players that had fallen down the pecking order.

One of the main positives of paying win money and loss money is that the players had to impress me enough in training and when they got their chance in games in order to keep their position. I mentioned very early on in the season that average performances simply weren't good enough to guarantee players a place in the team the following week. This wasn't a particular tactic of mine to get the best out of the players, I was just being honest and up front with them all and I think that they respected this approach.

With a large squad at my disposal and with no reserve team to draw on, it was always going to be difficult managing the players who weren't getting a spot in the team, but one of my strengths, I think, was integrity. I stood by my word. There were bound to be players unhappy at points in the season but my approach was always the same for everybody and I would always assure anybody that was unhappy that I wouldn't have signed them to the club if I didn't think they were talented. They knew they had to train hard and wait for their chance.

As for the players taking the field, they had bought into the systems I had put into place and, although we weren't able to maintain consistency on a week-to-week basis, we showed throughout the season what a talented bunch of players we had.

Looking back on the season in full, we could all be very happy with what was produced, but we could also be a little unhappy that we could have done so much better in certain games. There were away matches that we just didn't turn up mentally, which was disappointing, and there were also more away games there for the taking that we threw away, and overall, our away form was very average indeed. Our home form however was the complete opposite and we ended the season with one of the best home records in the division.

It was this form that saw us maintain a play-off position for the majority of the season and at times at Spotland we played some fantastic attacking rugby. The season ended with a loss to Blackpool at Fylde in the elimination game after we had finished fifth in the league and beaten South Wales Scorpions by 60 points, we could be proud of our achievements both on the field and off it and I certainly had no regrets about joining the club the previous October.

In 'the real world' of work, I had spent the previous eight months working as a lecturer in Warrington at Priestley College and I had been disappointed to learn that I wasn't being kept on past the summer holidays. I had taken the short term position the previous November knowing that the opportunity could possibly lead to a career, or be cut short by the return of the teacher I was covering, who was on maternity leave. Unfortunately for me, it ended up being the latter, and again I found myself without a full-time job.

There was a brief positive to come out of this situation, as I was able to concentrate fully at the back end of the season on a strong finish with Rochdale, which certainly had an impact on us going as far as we did in the play-offs. Our final game of the season came in early September and although we hadn't won promotion, everybody involved at the club was proud of our achievements. We could look back and pinpoint things we could have done better and games we could have probably won, but for this in-experienced group of players the season had been a big learning curve and one which would only make us stronger for 2011.

We finalised the season with one final but brief meet in the changing rooms after the defeat to Blackpool and I thanked the players and staff for their efforts throughout the year, before giving them details of when the process would all begin again. We would return to training on November 1st but, for now, the players and staff had a chance to enjoy a six-week break which had been well earned, but for me, it was straight into building for next season.

For as long as I have been involved in Rugby League, I have never been able to switch off. Whether it has been as a full-time player, full-time coach or even now as a part-time coach, I have found it difficult to think anything other than rugby. I could be sitting watching TV and a training drill will pop into my head out of nowhere. This can have its positives I suppose, but it can also have some negatives that can cause problems at home. I have been guilty in the past of putting too much time into my planning and preparation, and not having enough time for the kids and Kerry and I'm sure that played its part in our separation.

I don't feel that there is any such role within modern-day professional sport as a part-time player or a part-time coach and, for somebody with as much drive and determination as me, I can't afford to only give a job part-time hours. I try to give the players as much feedback as possible after games and this regularly means me staying up until the early hours of Monday morning to prepare video clips from the recent game to show the players. I am also guilty of spending a lot of time planning my sessions and there is a lot of thought that goes into them. There has to be. It's not just a case of turning up at training with notes scribbled onto a scrap piece of paper, everything is planned thoroughly. I try to be as professional in my approach to work as I possibly can be and I like to think that has an impact on the players I am working with. I am as much a part of the team as they are, and when the going gets tough, we are all in it together just as we are when things are working well.

You have to be resilient as a head coach and, at times, your patience is tested and things don't run as smoothly as you would have liked. But any coach will tell you that this is the fun of coaching, and if you prepare you players in the right way then you can hope for the best at the weekends on the pitch.

I often ask players, whether they are my own, or others that I meet from time to time, what their own interpretation is of the word 'professional', and I am regularly surprised to hear that some think it about getting paid. I like to think that when I recruit a player, or scout a young lad, they have the right attitude and work ethic and, for me, this is what being professional is all about. I often think back to my time as a player, and I always tried to behave in a professional way. I think I achieved this. I try to instil the same characteristics in my own players, but I can fully appreciate that part-time players who are currently playing the game at a 'professional' level will want to earn as much money as possible.

It is a short career, and one which isn't as well paid for the regular players as a lot of people think it is and, in my opinion, the players aren't paid enough. There aren't many players in the modern-day game that will be able to finish playing on their own terms and be able to hang up their boots and play golf for the rest of their lives. The likelihood is that players will have to get out there into the real world and find a job and, as I have experienced myself, it is easier said than done.

I have lots of personal regrets from the last fifteen years and I often think back and consider how my life could have been different should I have followed in the footsteps of my mate and got an apprenticeship after leaving school, but I'm not one for ifs and buts, and I am now living the life that I was dealt.

It certainly hasn't been easy and, at times, it has been incredibly difficult and it's at those times that you need the support of the people and the organisations you have worked with before. People often say, 'it's not what you know, it's who you know' and I believe this one hundred per cent. If you have the contacts, then nine times out of ten you will land on your feet, but if you don't have that network to fall back on in times of trouble, then who do you look to for support and help?

There have been tragedies that have happened quite recently and the circumstances surrounding Terry Newton's death in 2010 spring to mind. Banned from the sport for two years and cast aside from the game was a player that had represented his country at the highest level and played a major part in the success at both Wigan and Bradford, but for him things went wrong. Terry must have been in a lonely place to decide on his own fate and he must have felt his eventual actions were his only way out. We have to ask ourselves as a sport, are we doing enough for former professionals of our game?

Chapter 16

AS I WRITE THE FINAL CHAPTER OF MY book, I find myself thinking a lot about the 'what ifs'. I try not to, and it's something that I tell my players at Rochdale Hornets not to do, dwell on the past, but it is incredibly hard when you still see former team-mates playing the game and doing really well.

Life for me now has a new focus and the past few years have seen me drift from one job to another. It's not through a lack of commitment at all, but more a lack of direction. I think I know what I am good at, and the people I have worked for in the last few years know what I am good at, but there is quite some distance between being good at something and enjoying it. I have spent time working as a lecturer at Priestley College in Warrington, which I found interesting and fulfilling for a while, but it wasn't something I felt that I could commit to long term. The money wasn't bad, and there was a pathway to earn more money and with it more responsibility, but I wasn't using my skills in that role to my own advantage.

I spent six months in recruitment, working with Reed, in Stockport, and really enjoyed this role and the buzz of working with clients and candidates on jobs, but again, although I was told I was doing really well, I couldn't envisage myself working in that environment until retirement age. So I left the position to concentrate on me. I don't know whether it is the lack of excitement that means I get bored quite quickly, or the fact that I know I won't ever be able to achieve a good wage in those roles, but I have found that the lack of direction has certainly been to the detriment of home life.

I have found myself numerous times behind on the rent payments and the bills are often paid later than they should be. The unemployed will often say there are no jobs out there, which is untrue, there are lots of jobs to be had, but what is obvious to me having spent a brief spell in recruitment, is that the jobs out there are not for the unemployed. They are primarily for those with extensive prior experience or for university graduates. I have no formal qualifications to put on my CV and although I have been successful in what I have done so far in my working life, dependant on what you consider by the word success, I have found myself asking whether I have any hope of getting a well-paid job outside of rugby with good prospects for the future, and ultimately something that interests me and ignites something inside.

I often ask myself if indeed I made the right career choices back in 1996 when I signed for St Helens or whether as a young man I was given enough guidance. I have plenty of experience of working and working damn hard, but for the roles that are advertised, companies want the experience. How do you get experience without first having a go at the job? I have found it very frustrating to apply for position after position and to not even get a reply and, to make matters worse, the replies received have been as confidence shattering as they possibly could be.

It is this that has given me the determination again to succeed on my own terms and to use my unique set of skills to build my own business.

Ask any professional sportsperson what they believe they possess as skills, and they will tell you that they have a tremendous work ethic, a commitment to achievement and a desire to be the best that they can be. After all, that is what makes them professionals. Now if those skills, as well as lots of dedication, are not desirable by employers then I don't know what is, and the frustrating part is that I know that I could do the majority of the jobs I have applied for, with my hands tied behind my back and blindfolded.

I know it isn't just me that has been in the predicament of unemployment after sport. If somebody would have told me I would have retired from playing the game through injury at the age of 25 then I wouldn't have believed them, but the reality is that for my commitment to become a Super League player, I paid a price. I left myself in an impossible position when it comes to finding a 'real' job. I have even applied for positions within call centres, simply answering telephones, and I have been unsuccessful, as I haven't had any call centre experience. I am a person who has represented the country at the highest sporting level and who has been a world champion, albeit from within a team, but for companies out there, this means nothing, I couldn't even get a £12,000 a year telesales job, even though I'm not sure I'd want to go down this route.

It is frightening however to think that I am now 31

years old and although I am carving out a career as a coach in rugby league, the doors to the other working industries seem closed or uninspiring, and with the responsibility of financially supporting my two children as well as trying to look after myself, it is no wonder I feel as vulnerable as I do.

I recently received a letter through the post, from St Helens County Court and my immediate reaction was that it was a summons, which gives you a bit of an idea of my current financial position and, of course, my mindset at present. It wouldn't be the first, and I'm sure it won't be the last that I receive, and through no particular fault of my own, but this particular letter was for the mind-blowing figure of £65,000! When my house my repossessed not long after I was forced to retire, the bank had to look for a new buyer in order to recover their losses, and their priority of a quick sale meant they sold at under market value. The policy then allowed them to bill me for the shortfall, and I am then called before the courts to arrange payment.

The reality of the situation is that I am very unlikely to be able to pay them any money at this moment in time or for that matter any time in the near future. In fact, I can't ever imagine I will be earning enough money again that will see me be able to come to an arrangement to repay the debt. Sometimes, it is hard to see any light at the end of the tunnel and, in my case, it seems far too often that I am getting closer to the end, and the builders are extending the tunnel.

Surprisingly, I am able to stay positive, although I

have a lot to probably be depressed about, but I put that down to my responsibilities as a father. I can't afford to let the negatives get the better of me and, in fact, I am a very positive person in general, but at times, I do wonder what I have done to deserve the things that have happened since my retirement. Sure, I have made some bad decisions like everybody else, but for now, at least in my personal life, the luck has deserted me. I'm just waiting for that opportunity to get myself back on an even footing.

You might be thinking to yourself that I should use the money that I put aside for the Spanish villa in order to repay all my debts, but unfortunately for me that is another area where I was hit hard. The Spanish property crash meant that my deposit was swallowed up in the resale value and although my dad manages to scrimp and scrape each month to keep his side of the mortgage ongoing, I was forced to cut my losses and move on from that particular investment without success.

It is these negatives that have inspired me to tell my story and to use my experiences to advise others on the perils that can take control if you aren't prepared to control your life properly. Sometimes people do make errors of judgement and the occasional bad decision, but I feel that preparation is the key. If you can prepare yourself in every area of your life then it makes it a whole lot harder to fail and whether that is through education or not, having a plan is important.

If I could have my time over, I would make

different choices for myself, but I can't afford to look back in anger, I must look forward to the future. I have two beautiful children and my one goal is to make sure that they want for nothing. It might take me a while, but I will get there in the end.

I have recently kick started my own business, JS Elite Performance and Training, which encompasses all of my experiences and life skills. I know that this business is a unique business that only I can offer as there is only me that has experienced the ups and the downs and all that goes with that. Within the business I am working with many different people from different walks of life, and whilst my passion is for sport, I am able to also offer individuals and companies my experiences of fear and motivation in order for them to improve. Some people call it being a 'life coach', and although I am only 31 years-old and I have much more of my life to live, I feel that I have experienced a life so far that can be used as an example to others in order to highlight the potential positives and negatives that are out there every day.

I am working with schools, local businesses, national companies, sports teams, sports individuals and fellow coaches so that I can influence in a posi-tive way. Quite often in life, it is good to sit back and get a reality check and although I have had plenty of those so far in my life, I'm not so sure that the young professionals of sport, specifically rugby league, have given much thought to anything other than sport. I was exactly the same as a young lad with my single mindedness and look where I am now, it's a lesson to be learned. I am also currently involved in a minor way in a project which has been launched by GPW Recruitment of St Helens and focuses on giving players the opportunity to work on day release for one day a week within local businesses. The aim of the business is simple in that we hope to give the lads a taste of working life and give them career options for when they do eventually finish playing.

I'm sure that the majority of them will see 'work' as a chore, and they will feel right now they will be able to play on forever. But the reality is that this simply won't happen and for the majority, when they put the boots on their peg for the last time, they won't have earned enough money to stop working altogether. Hopefully though, through the 'Rugby League Recruitment' project, they will take advantage of this fantastic opportunity and they will build some relationships with local firms or educate themselves to a level that will see them prosper in later years. They will also have hopefully had a taste of working in different sectors that will give them definite work pathways for when the time comes.

I only wish that there had been something like this available when I first started to break through at St Helens and maybe I would have been able to move on with my life when I finished playing. For now, things are slow and I am currently bringing in just over a thousand pounds per month to satisfy outgoings of nearly double that figure, so you can see where the problem lies. But as I write, I have been lucky enough to meet a man called Andy Preston who is recognised worldwide as the leading sales trainer in the world. A chance meeting with Andy at a rugby union dinner gave me the opportunity to explain my own vision to him for my future and he has given me the opportunity to work alongside him to build up my sales experience. The opportunity that presents is one I cannot let pass me by, and there is a plan in place for me to eventually take advantage of my experience and speak to companies about sports recruitment and motivation. As my business starts to grow, and my name becomes more well known in the business world I will able to spread my message to those who are wise enough to listen.

That message is that ultimately, as my mum has always said, the person that you can rely on the most to help yourself is you.